JUNIOR SAINTS

JUNIOR SAINTS

THE RICH RARE HUMOR
OF KIDS IN CHURCH

Compiled By
Oren Arnold

KREGEL PUBLICATIONS
Grand Rapids, Michigan 49501

Library of Congress Catalog Card Number 75-12108
ISBN 0-8254-2117-9

FIRST EDITION

Printed in the United States of America

DEDICATED

With love to our own three "angels", who outwitted Adele and me so constantly and almost wrecked the church, yet somehow grew up into true Christian womanhood; also, to their husbands and their angelic — Iusethetermloosely — children who now outwit their grandparents and parents and pastors, hence in their turn are enlivening the tabernacles. These happy, uninhibited, sharp-minded folk are, in the order of their appearance:

JUDY, and Pat	ROSIE, and Jerry	GAIL, and Bob
Robin	Randy	Ricky
Erin	Davey	Wendy
	Sharie	
	Larry	

*"Every child proves that God
is not discouraged with man."*

THE TREASURY

For twenty years or so I have written regular pages of humor in several magazines, including at intervals such distinguished journals as *Better Homes and Gardens, Household, Woman's Day, Your Life, Sunday Digest, Presbyterian Life,* and the big Baptist *Home Life.* These have stimulated thousands of readers to mail in the funny incidents, anecdotes, jokes and stories developed spontaneously at churches across the continent.

The best — the very richest and most enjoyable church-related humor — is the "Oh-dear-whatever-shall-we-do-with-him!" kind that Junior generates, the "Sister-darling-how-could-you!" kind that completely upsets Mother but delights Grandpop and the minister. That treasury is collected in this volume.

Keep in mind that nobody is being irreverent here; nobody is ridiculing the church or showing any kind of disrespect for its sacred aspects. It's just that man has a sense of humor. I am quite sure that God himself has one — He made us in His image, didn't He?

Our beloved children activate it most of all.

Oren Arnold

CONTENTS

1

THE ADORABLE INNOCENTS

Ah, the innocence of the innocents — how marvelous it is! It makes them literal minded and credulous (never mind what this does to the parents). It also generates endless fine malapropisms. Such as that of the youngster who slightly confused an old hymn by singing "How strong and sweet my father's cane." And another from the lad who garbled the involvements of royalty by reporting that "Solomon had forty porcupines."

A favorite is the fortunate misunderstanding of the little girl who recited the twenty-third Psalm, "The Lord is my shepherd. That's all I want." That's all *I* want, too, sweetie; matter of fact, that's all any of us needs. And certainly she was more theological than the other little girl who ended The Lord's Prayer with this, "For thine is the kingdom, and the flowers that are growing. Amen." But come to think of it, she wasn't too far wrong either.

Let us, then, approach our junior saints by studying their lovable, literal, little minds, and watch the dawning of imagination and exploration as we move along. We can start right back with the first woman.

+

This was one of those beautiful old family Bibles. You know the kind — eight inches thick, full of birth records and such, but best of all, smudged from much reading. It had been around for generations. Modern little Suzanne discovered it one day, and deep inside it she found a large and pretty leaf that must have been pressed there by some 1890 sentimentalist.

Suzy ran with it to the living room, eyes bright, "Grandmommy, look what I found in your Bible! Do you suppose it was worn by Eve?"

+

Literal and logical? Certainly our kids are. "What did the Israelites do," the preacher asked a group of small fry, "after they walked through the Red Sea?"

"Well," Bobby answered, "I guess they dried theirselfs."

+

Or how about the equally observant little Rosie Arnold, age five. Her logic should be inspiring for all of us. One brilliantly starlit evening she looked upward and said to her family in the patio, "Oh, what a wonderful place heaven must be, when its underside is so beautiful!"

+

Less poetic, but surely no less accurate, was this report from little Robert Watson.

"What happens to a man," the kindly minister asked him, "who never thinks of his soul, but pays attention only to his body?"

You grown-up gents give heed to Bobby's answer — "He gets fat."

Little minds do get mixed up at times. The very dour and dignified Reverend Dr. Pompous Pontificate had stalked into the Sunday School room. He asked a class of small children if they could tell him anything about Peter, and one little girl instantly held up her hand. "Very well," said he, loftily, "you may tell us about him. Speak up loudly so all can hear."

She spoke up loudly: *"Peter, Peter, pumpkin eater, had a wife and couldn't keep her."*

So that took care of that. Next question?

+

Dr. Pontificate scowled his way back to dignity, and inasmuch as this was mid-March, he warily asked the class, "Who can tell me something about Good Friday?"

Imagine the poor preacher's reaction when one eager-beaver lad almost shouted a correct answer, "I can sir. He was Robinson Crusoe's right-hand man and friend!"

+

Tense and furious now, Dr. Pontificate also was hard-headed. He would ask a question that had no possible misinterpretation. So — "Who was Goliath?" he rumbled. His expression seemed to dare the children to make something of this one.

But, ah ha, little Elizabeth Hall meditated a moment then piped up, "I think he was the man David rocked to sleep."

+

This preacher called at the home. Ten-year-old

Erin welcomed him, and he promptly began to question her. "Do you come regularly to Sunday School, Erin?"

"Yes sir, I sure do," she nodded.

"Good, good. And do you know the Bible?"

Mother trembled a bit here, but Erin remained poised. "Oh yes, sir, I know it."

"Excellent, my dear." The minister was pleased. "Possibly you could tell me something that is in it?"

"Yes sir, I can tell you everything that's in it."

Now that was a broad claim! The man himself couldn't have claimed so much. Of course he pursued the matter.

"Can you really! Do tell me then."

"Well, " said Erin, ticking off items on her finger, "there's an old tintype picture of grandmother's grandmother, and a lock of my hair, and mama's diet for reducing, and two pawn tickets for father's watch and ring."

+

"Why don't you come to my church with me?" said 6-year-old Davey to his friend Chuck.

"Because," explained Chuck, *"I belong to another abomination."*

+

We oldsters ourselves don't always grasp those intricate Bible teachings, so let none of us feel superior to little Martha Malloy. Her preacher, talking to the children, explained about Elijah. It seems that Elijah built an altar and put wood on it. Then Elijah cut a bullock into pieces (*that* took some explaining, too!) and put the pieces on the wood on the altar. Next, Elijah ordered the people to pour four barrels of water over the pieces of bullock on the wood on the altar. (That does sound like a lot of water).

At this point the preacher asked the children, "Now why did Elijah want water poured over the bullock?"

The answer is obvious, of course; at least it was to sweet little Martha, who often helped her mommy in the kitchen at home. Said she, "To make the gravy!"

+

The juvenile group was gathered closely in the back yard, and Mother of course asked, "What are you doing, whispering that way?"

"Playing church," one child replied.

"Worshipers do not whisper in church," said Mother.

"Oh," the observant innocents explained, "but we are the choir."

+

In sixth grade at school young James wrote a composition about the Quaker faith. He wrote that Quakers are mighty fine people (which, of course, is true). He explained that they never spoke harshly, never quarreled, never attacked one another or tried to claw or fight or be ill tempered, never demanded anything unreasonable. It was a good composition, and deserved the A grade that it got. Perhaps the most interesting point that he made was one tagged on as as afterthought, "My Papa is a Quaker. My Mama is not."

Six-year-old Sharon had recently been baptized. Her father asked her if she wished to attend church. "Yes," said she, "And let's take new baby brother Larry and get him advertized like me."

+

Ricky Turek had been twice to church. Evidently he listened more closely than his parents expected, especially last Sunday when the minister preached on the creation, telling how Eve was made after Adam had a pain in his side.

So next Tuesday when Ricky got a sudden pain in his own side after running too far too fast, he ran to his mother, reported the ailment, then wailed, "Do you suppose I am going to have a wife?"

+

Because it was a special day for children, Willie went to big church this morning. When he came home he was accosted by Mother, who was always suspicious anyhow. "William, did you behave in church?"

"Sure I did!" He looked indignantly at her. "Why the lady right behind me told another lady she had never seen a boy behave so!"

+

Little Charlotte was bragging. "My daddy is a doctor. I can be sick for nothing."

Her friend Leslie shot back. "My daddy is a preacher. I can be good for nothing."

Four-year-old Roy watched his father gulp two pills at Sunday breakfast, a routine ritual, then announced that "Moses had indigestion just like you do, Pop."

Pop frowned and asked, "Now how would you know that?"

"The preacher said God gave Moses two tablets."

+

They had buried the elderly gentleman just yesterday, after a long and happy 89 years. Today sweet little Bessie Lou was rummaging in a dresser drawer, when she let out a cry — "Oh Mother, Great-Granddaddy has gone to heaven without his glasses, and he won't be able to see a thing!"

+

Maybe you heard about the new recruit for the church's junior basketball team? No? Well, he went home and told his mother he had to have a big P sewed on his jersey. When she asked why, he explained, "Because I am playing with the Piscopalians."

+

"On the Day of Judgment," nine-year-old Tommy wrote on his test paper, "some will be re-united with their loved ones, others with their wives."

+

Strange animals roam the wilds of America and American juvenile imaginations. "I want to see the cross-eyed bear," little Susan demanded after church one Sunday.

"Whatever are you talking about?" her daddy fumed. "There's no such animal."

"There is too, so. In church we even sang about the concentrated cross-eyed bear."

+

Miss Minerva Weems the choir soprano never "rendered" a solo without shaking her head up and down unnecessarily. Little Michelee stood it as long as she could, and when Miss Minerva came to a moment of silence, a pause in the music, sweet M'lee piped out, "Mother, she could sing better if she'd stop bobbing for apples."

+

The fatuous preacher was trying to be cheery. "Well, well, Cindy," said he to the little girl, "I hear that you have a baby brother at your house. Are you happy about that?"

"I don't like him?" Cindy declared.

"Oh, and why not?"

"'Cause he's all red and squirmy and noisy."

The pastor smiled big. "Then why don't you send him back?"

Cindy was tempted by the thought, but finally shrugged and replied, "I guess not. We have already used him three days."

+

2

HEAVEN BOUND

The country preacher had to go to New York on business, so he took his little boy along to show him the sights. Of course, they had to go to the top of the Empire State building.

Z-Z-z z z z went the elevator, swishing them upward. The little fellow's stomach tightened, his ears popped. He was deeply impressed; he was sure they would never stop ascending. When they paused for a moment at the 68th floor, he startled all the passengers by demanding loudly, "Father, does God know we are coming?"

+

Rosemary, the mother, had been working hard to teach her children correct grammar. "You must say, 'I haven't *any*,'" she kept telling them. "Don't say 'I haven't none.'"

Well and good. But next Sunday they passed a Catholic church and saw two nuns crossing the churchyard. "Look," Sharie said to her brother, "there go two anys."

+

"Remember," little Becky told her brother Chris, "you are not allowed to talk in church. They won't let you."

Six-year-old Chris demanded, "Who won't let me?"

Said Becky, "The hushers won't let you, that's who."

+

Twelve-year-old Thomas had been given a wrist watch that had an alarm. Sure enough, it happened! The Reverend Dr. William Boice had just five more sentences to go on his magnificent sermon, the congregation was rapt with silence, when — *BRIN-N-N-N-NG!* You could have heard it a block away.

Mother, sitting beside Tom, jumped half out of her skin and reached for that watch. She couldn't find the shut-off knob. She began slapping the watch and wrist, *WHAP, WHAP, WHAP,* trying to stop the ringing. No success.

"Never mind, Thomas," said kindly Dr. Boice. "My sermon has just pointed up an alarming situation in our world, and you have just emphasized it for me. I thank you for your help. Now let us bow for the benediction."

+

In church the little boy was running his toy railroad engine up and down the back of the pew in front. Crotchety elderly Mr. Pedrick turned around to him and said "Sh-h-h, Sh-h!"

The little boy piped up, "Oh, do you play trains too?"

+

In Dallas, Texas, little Tessie was taken to church one day and saw the people all dressed up in dark clothes and being very serious. She asked her mother a question that all of us pseudo-Christians might well ask ourselves, "Mother, where do Christians stay all week? I see them only when I go to church."

+

The preacher, lecturing the children, said, "Lot was ordered to take his wife and daughters and flee out of Sodom. Now does anyone have any questions?"

Of course, somebody did. One wee person held up a hand and with a lisp asked, "Pleath, thir, how old wath the flee?"

+

Here's another one with a moral for all of us hardened adults. The preacher saw little Alice approaching, and knew that her family was in the process of moving from one dwelling to another. Smiling, he said, "Well, Alice, I hear that you don't have any home these days."

"Oh yes, sir, we have a home." she assured him earnestly. "We just don't have a house to put it in."

+

Again it was close to Christmas. The fine stories had been read and enjoyed once more, the beloved carols sung. So, little four-year-old Louise piped up, "Mommy, wasn't it nice for the sheep men to clean themselves all up before they visited the baby Jesus."

Of course Mommy had to ask, "What do you mean, dear?"

"Well it says in the song 'While shepherds washed their socks by night.'"

The little girl was born and raised in very arid Arizona. She had never seen an ocean, but her minister father kept promising to take her to the California coast. Eventually he was able to do so. The parents took her to the water's edge at Laguna Beach, where great waves were crashing dramatically and noisily.

"Oh Mommy," exclaimed the sweetiepie, "God made us such a wonderful ocean! I just love it. Especially when it flushes!"

+

Mother took little Shirley Goodwin to church for the first time. She listened attentively to everything, and Mother wondered what she might have gotten out of the long service. At home, Mother got the answer. Shirley ran from the car to her Father, shouting, "Daddy, Daddy, I am in the Bible!"

"Oh, how is that, sweetheart?"

"The preacher read it out loud. He said 'Shirley Goodwin and mercy shall follow me all the days of my life!'"

+

A little girl was given a new teddy bear to cuddle in bed. She noticed that one eye seemed crooked, "But it's all right, Mommy. I'll just name him Gladly."

Mother was surprised. "Isn't that an odd name for a bear?"

"Oh no." The child was positive. "It's even in a church song. Last Sunday we sang it, 'Gladly, my cross-eyed bear.'"

A Chicago minister was describing the Day of Judgment. Seems it will be quite an occasion — "The sky will open," said the good preacher. "Thunder will crash, earthquakes will rock the universe, lightning will flash everywhere, the sun will turn pale, buildings will topple and mountains will move." He made a vivid description.

When he paused for dramatic effect, one little girl spoke out loudly in the moment of silence, "Mother, will I get out of school?"

The class of Junior boys was putting up a Nativity scene in the front of the church. One turned to ask the preacher, "Sir, where shall I put the Three Wise Guys?"

+

The wonderful, kindly, old physician was loved by everybody in the church, for he had healed many people and comforted many more. Then he himself died, and the parish grieved. Next day the little son of the minister asked, "Daddy, is God very sick?"

"Sick?" The preacher showed his surprise. "Certainly not, son. God is never sick. Why would you ask that?"

"Well when Dr. Morris died, I thought God must have sent for him."

+

The church yard needed mowing, and enterprising ten-year-old Horace applied for the job; said he wanted to mow it every week. The preacher feeling foxy today anyway, smiled and said, "Well now, Horace, we must discuss your pay. Tell me, what would you do with a million dollars?"

Harold's brow furrowed in thought. "I don't know, sir. Anyway I wouldn't want that much at the start."

+

The congregation was repeating the famous Twenty-third Psalm. At the end of it, little Larry yelped, "You left out the hair oil part!" He seemed so distressed that his daddy Jerry whispered an inquiry, "Which part, son?" Replied Larry, "Thou anointest my head with oil, my cup runneth over."

In a Vacation Bible School, each child in the class of little folks was drawing a picture to illustrate the grand song *America The Beautiful.* The preacher happened in and young Butch showed him his artistic effort — a field of yellow corn, purple mountains, blue skies and such.

"But," said the preacher, "what's this thing like an airplane all covered with bananas, oranges and grapes?"

"Oh," explained Butch, "that's the fruited-plane."

+

The very little girl wandered into the big church. An usher, unable to find her parents, escorted her to a pew and whispered, "Sit there for the present."

When Mother did arrive, the church happened to be absolutely quiet. So the little girl was heard to say, "A man told me to sit here for the present, but he never did bring me any present."

+

The Reverend Dr. Charles Ehrhardt is a poetic soul, who sees God in almost everything good. So he took small daughter out into the fields one autumn to watch the migration of the birds. Sure enough a large gathering of mallard ducks seemed about ready to take off, with much quacking and "talking."

Said the preacher, "What do you suppose they are saying to one another, darling?"

Little Janet drew from experience. "Most likely the mama ducks are telling the young ones to go to the bathroom before they start."

 Little Jennifer, sitting in the church pew with her mother, began to feel queasy. "Mother," she whispered desperately, "I think I have to frow up."

"Oh dear!" Mother didn't want to cause a commotion here. She whispered back, "Slip out the front door and run into the garden."

Jennifer hastened out, but was back in a few moments. "Back so soon?" Mother whispered.

"Yes. I didn't have to go outside the building at all."

"But Jenny!"

"It's all right, Mother. They have a little box on a stand right inside the church door. I just lifted the lid and . . ."

"Jenny!"

But they *do,* Mommy! It has a sign on it, 'For The Sick.'"

+

Tall Reverend Mr. George Patterson was walking down the street, holding the hand of his little son, when a large dog trotted toward them. Sonny turned to run, but father held him. "Do not be afraid of dogs, my boy," said the kindly man.

Sonny sniffled. "B-But you'd be a-afraid t-too, if you were as l-low down as I am!"

+

Little Margie had been baptized when aged six. Next Friday the preacher happened to be walking by her house. Margie said to her playmate, "There's the man who capsized me."

3

FORKED TAILS

Of course, of course, certainly, children are made in heaven. Regrettably, a lot of them while here on earth, seem to get a bit of training from the other place. These are the ones who develop horns and forked tails.

Some of them must have gotten at the baptismal font at a church in Riverside, California, one morning. At any rate when the sacred moment came, elder Brown swung back the hand-carved lid, the pastor dipped his fingers into the liquid and dribbled it impressively onto the very blonde head of Miss Laura B-----.

In the dim light there, nobody noticed until too late that a dark green indelible ink had been poured into the water.

+

The Ladies Aid Society was holding its weekly meeting this afternoon in the home of Mrs. Gail Turek. Sixteen ladies, plus the preacher, were present in full dignity. Very young Wendy Lee Turek walked in the front door, all dressed up and beaming. Mother Gail smiled benignly and spoke to her darling.

"Oh, you are home from the children's party. Tell us, dear, what mother's little sweetie did there." It would be so cute to hear, no doubt.

Replied Miss Wendy, "I frowed up."

And how about the little flower girl at Rosie Arnold's marryin'? Her name was Ruth Ann. She looked cute as pie in her specially-made dress. She was back there at the door, waiting with her basket of rose petals. On cue from the organ, the bride's father pushed her forward, saying, "Now, darling, go on down the aisle and throw your flowers."

Nobody had ever told sweet Ruth Ann *how* to throw those rose petals. But she had recently been at a church carnival where the children all threw confetti, so naturally she drew on experience now.

She leaped high, tossing handfuls of rose petals far out over the pews and onto the heads of wedding guests! Never a one on the carpeted aisle for the bride to walk on.

+

The dignified and distinguished Reverend Dr. Evermore Thredbaire had come to the home as a dinner guest. The family had seated him and themselves at table, when mother noticed an omission. She stagewhispered to her helper, little Mildred Nell, "Why didn't you put a knife and fork at Dr. Thredbaire's place, darling?"

Millienell had a logical though devilish answer, "I thought he wouldn't need them. Daddy says he always eats like a horse."

+

Forked-tailed spirits do get around. Two little girl neighbors and friends had developed one whale of a fight this morning. Mary's mother separated them, then severely scolded her daughter, "Shame on you, Mary. I'm sure it was Satan who suggested that you push Alice and pull her hair."

"No doubt it was," agreed Mary solemnly. "But I can tell you one thing — kicking her in the stomach was my own idea!"

Very possibly, those same naughty boys (or girls?) were first cousins of the ones in Houston, Texas, who *quietly* poured a gallon of concentrated detergent into the Baptist church baptistry. Nothing showed until the pastor led Miss Marsha Lee into the liquid for immersion. But their swishing motions were just enough to erupt suds all over the glass rim and down onto the heads of the choir members!

Monday night was Daddy's night off. Daddy, the preacher, Junior, and his mother sat on the living room floor, thumbing through the old family photo album. They come onto a picture of a handsome, slim, young man with a full head of black hair and a black mustache.

"Who's he?" asked Junior.

"That's your father, dear," replied Mother.

"That?" exclaimed Junior. "Then who is the fat bald-headed man who has been living with us?"

+

In Everett, Washington, the big church choir was walking down the aisle in stately processional, wearing their white robes. At a pause between verses of their song, little Bart Duggan yelped out, "Look, Mommy, they are all going to get their hair cut!"

+

In this church, a Mr. Hornbuckle, aged 81, got bored with the Reverend Mr. Jager's sermon, and did what comes naturally; he put his head back on the pew and went to sleep.

Unfortunately, his mouth came wide open there. In the balcony, on the front row were two boys, also bored. They saw that open mouth. Using the paper bulletin they made spit balls, and then —

You guessed it.

+

In Patterson, New Jersey, a Sunday School teacher asked for pencil drawings of King David. She got six showing him wearing a coonskin cap.

The wedding ceremony was under way. The bride walked sedately down the aisle — step pause step, step pause step, with her little sister demurely holding the long train of lace. But right there near the altar, the moppet's foot happened to strike a potted plant. The thing went *crack* and dirt spilled as the plant rolled ten feet or so, scattering flowers.

"That," said the little girl to her sister the bride, loudly enough for all the church to hear, "was a stinky place to stick a lily."

+

Now here is that famous apocryphal story of the little boy who was on the front porch, on tiptoes, trying to reach a doorbell. The kindly minister happened to be passing, so he said, "Here, my little man, let me help you," and he himself rang the bell.

The boy grinned big, looked up at his helper, and suggested, "Okay mister, now run like mad," and took to his heels.

+

Young Willard had brought a gift to the pastor's home from his mother. "Thank you very much, Willard," said the man. "I will call tomorrow and thank your mother also, for these eight large red apples."

Willard hesitated a moment then pleaded, "Sir, would you please thank her for twelve big red apples?"

+

 The good clergyman's little daughter stubbed her toe and uttered a swear word.

Papa heard it, but remained calm. "Sweetheart," said he, "I will give you ten cents if you will never, never say that word again."

Three days later she came to him and said, "Daddy, I've got a word that's worth fifty cents."

+

The preacher heard a commotion out back of the church just after Sunday School. He went out there, found two boys fighting, and of course stopped them.

"Couldn't you two lads settle your differences," said he, sternly, "by a peaceful discussion, calling in the assistance of an unprejudiced opinion if necessary?"

One boy shrugged. "No sir. He was so sure he could whip me, and I was so sure I could whip him, and there was only one way to find out who was right."

+

In Drexel Hill, Pennsylvania, J.M. Minster was relaxing in his yard one balmy Sunday afternoon when two small neighbor lads wandered in.

"Did you boys go to church today?" the gentleman asked.

One said, "yes". But little Ozzie said, "no".

"Why didn't you go, Ozzie? The guardian angel may neglect to watch over you next week."

Oz worried about that a moment, then asked, "Is he coming next week?"

The small boy with glasses was, of course, super-intelligent. (All boys who wear glasses are; it is their compensation for being unable to play football). As an avid reader he said to his preacher one day, "Sir, I don't think Solomon was nearly as rich as you said he was in your sermon."

"Why don't you think so, Harold?" the good man asked.

"Well, the Bible says that he slept with his fathers. If he had all that money you said he had, surely he would have bought a bed for himself."

+

Six-year-old Carol was visiting Grandma, and helping set the supper table. "What are we having to eat?" she asked.

"Fish, dear," replied Grandma.

"Why do we have fish every Friday when I visit you?"

"Because we belong to a church that believes in eating fish on certain days, sweetheart."

Carol gave thought to that, then ruled, "When I grow up, I am going to join a hamburger church."

+

After all these years, Eve is still fouling up things.

"Richard Turek!" snapped Mrs. Robert Turek one day, to her six-year-old son, "Why did you hit your sister?"

Rich had explanation for that, which we can say completely exonerated him. "We were playing Adam and Eve with an apple, and instead of tempting me with it, she ate it all up herself."

The preacher and his wife, out for an evening, came home late and she said to her baby sitter, "Did you have any trouble with Junior? Usually he is as good as gold."

Replied the sitter, "Well shortly after you left, he went off the gold standard."

+

An outdoorsman father had a den in his home. His little girl Judy loved to play in there, and today she was pretending to be a doctor, having all her play equipment for it scattered. Presently she picked it all up in her black "doctor bag" and hastened out, leaving the den door open.

"Judith," called father from his desk, "come back and close the door."

She pretended not to hear him, so he repeated his command loudly. Finally she trudged back, slammed the door shut and went on off. But soon she was back, looking dejected. The kindly father smiled and asked, "How is your patient getting along?"

"He died," cried Judy angrily, "while I was closing that door."

+

This allegedly took place at the big Union Station in Los Angeles. Little Susie got lost from her mother. Mom searched frantically, finally found her in the midst of a group of black-and-white clad nuns.

"Oh Sisters!" Mom exlaimed. "I do hope Susan wasn't annoying you!"

"Not at all," one of the nuns replied. "In fact she was enjoying herself. She seems to think we are penguins."

4

TARNISHED HALOS

Tough young Rocky O'Hara, age six, doubtless wore his forked tail and his horns to Sunday School this morning but left his halo at home. In the playroom, he got on the new hobby horse and monopolized it. Other kids howled for a turn on it, but he stayed fast in the saddle.

The teacher pleaded. He wouldn't get off.

The preacher happened in and he pleaded, then tried to lift Rock off. Rock clung on tight, grinning. "Giddy-yap!" he shouted.

No persuasion from anybody could get him off. Then the church janitor, another Irishman, happened to enter the room, and learned the cause of the commotion.

"Leave it to me," said the janitor quietly.

He walked over to Rocky on that horse, whispered in his ear. The child gave him a startled glance, dismounted at once, walked over to his pastor, and fearfully took him by the hand as if for protection. The pastor took Rocky to his mother but soon returned, full of curiosity.

"Whatever did you say to that boy to make him get off the horse?" he asked the janitor.

"Oh, not much," the janitor shrugged it off. "I just whispered to him, 'You ornery brat, if you are not off that horse in ten seconds, I'm going to knock your block off!'"

+

 This was a few nights before Christmas, which Robin, age ten, and Erin, age six, were spending with grandparents. At bedside prayers, Erin was heard to petition the Lord in loud tones, "And please God let Santa Claus bring me two new dolls and a kitchen play set and a bike and a pony and a doll buggy and lots of candy and a pretty new dress and some skates and a coloring book and a lot of . . .

"Sh-h-h-h-h," interrupted older sister Robin. "You don't need to pray so loud. God is not deaf."

"No," explained Erin, low tone, "but Grand-daddy is."

+

The Reverend Dr. George Hunter Hall approached young hotshot gradeschooler, Don Creamer, of his flock. "Donald, I have just learned that your uncle is a mortician. I thought you told me he was a doctor."

"Oh, no, sir," declared Don. "I simply said he followed the medical profession."

+

Halos get tarnished because they are flagrantly left unpolished by wearers such as young Buster Malloy.

In this instance, the preacher had come to visit. He was sitting stiffly in the parlor sipping coffee with the lady of the house. Everything was sedate and formal and dignified; until boisterous Buster came clumping down the stairway, as if he were a ten-ton truck. He saw the minister, grinned devilishly, and said, "Sorry about that, Chief."

Mother immediately scolded, ending with an order, "You march yourself right back up those stairs and come down quietly."

He slank, slunk? out, but was back in two minutes. "Did you hear me that time, Mom?" he asked.

"No, that was much better. Now you understand what it is to act like a dignified little gentleman."

"Sure thing. This time I slid down the banister!"

The sisters of citizens like Buster don't do much toward keeping halos polished, either. Now you take little Merrilee Hale, daughter of a minister. She had just celebrated her sixth birthday, and for it Mother gave her a big bottle of cheap but flashily-packed perfume, and Father gave her a cheap but operable wrist watch.

Miss Merry was duly impressed. She doused herself generously and trotted all over the neighborhood, exuding fragrance and making people listen to her watch tick; finally her mother had to stop it.

"Merrilee," said she, severely, "we are having the church Elders and their wives for dinner tonight, and I don't want you to say a thing about your gifts. Do you hear?"

Merry nodded glumly. She obeyed her Mommy until the dinner conversation was well under way. Then, choosing a quiet moment, she said, "If anybody hears anything or smells anything, it's me."

Or how about little Janet? She hadn't wanted to go to bed in the first place. (Does any child ever want to go to bed?) But her father was the church organist, and her mother was the choir director, so they were strict. Even so, this night Miss Janet bluffed and made excuses and talked and pleaded. But finally mother got her to bed, turned out the light, and left Janet alone.

Three minutes passed, and Janet called out. "Mother-er, it's too dark in here. I'm scared."

"Oh hush, darling. Just be still and go to sleep. Remember, the angels are in there with you."

Two minutes more passed. "Mother-er!"

"Now what?"

"Mother, one of the angels just bit me!"

In St. Paul, Minnesota, eleven-year-old Junior Ewald had just broken his third hockey stick in one season. Dad had already scolded him about breaking the other two, so now the boy trudged home with great apprehension.

Happily, the pastor had just come to call, and was sitting with Dad and Mother. Junior grasped opportunity by the forelock, "Dad, this is a good time to tell you that I accidently broke my hockey stick."

+

The Saturday afternoon party for the children at the church was a fine success. Many rich refreshments were served, some left over. "Do have something more, Oswald," the hostess said to one small lad.

"No, thank you," said he. "I am full."

"Well, then put some cakes and fruit in your pockets to eat on the way home," she urged.

"Can't. They're full, too."

+

The Saturday church luncheon was under way, with many mothers and children present. Accustomed to thick he-man sandwiches such as were put in her father's lunch box, little Cathie was puzzled when she encountered her first pink-tea style sandwiches.

"Whoever cut the bread for these?" she asked, loudly.

The preacher's wife, pleased at what she assumed would be a compliment, replied, "Why I did, darling."

"Well," said Cathie, "you almost missed it."

+

This was a Community Church, and the time was Christmas, so reports D.J. Peterson of Los Angeles. Each department had its tableau to present as part of the birthday celebration. In one scene four kindergarten kids were to hold up big cards that spelled out STAR.

For the audience, it turned out much better than the teacher had dared hope. With music swelling, those four kids somehow got themselves mixed up and the sign read RATS.

+

 Reverend Dr. Speakwell heard that the Smith family had new triplets and met little Jimmy Smith on the street. "James," he began, "I am told that the stork has smiled on your home."

"Smiled!" snorted Jimmy. " He laughed out loud!"

+

"What was the greatest surprise of your life?" the preacher asked a ten-year-old boy.

Replied the lad, "When I sneaked under a circus tent, and found myself in a church revival meeting."

+

Rich woman, showing off her diamonds to tough young John Howard, age twelve, "Have you seen the two diamond rings my husband gave to me for my birthday?"

John shot from the hip. "yes, I saw them when you put that nickel in the collection plate Sunday."

"I hear God sent you two more little brothers, Carol," said the kindly preacher.

"Yeah, and He also knows where the money is coming from to feed them. I heard Daddy say so."

+

The old gentleman was quizzing the minister's small son — "Georgie, does your father ever preach the same sermon twice?"

"Oh yes, sir," agreed Georgie, "but he hollers in different places."

+

Sweet and innocent little Mary discovered her mother's open purse. Just when she seemed about to filch a hand full of coins, mother herself was seen approaching.

Mary closed the purse quickly, smiled at her mother, and said, "The devil sure isn't getting very far with *me* these days, is he?"

+

Six-year-old Charlotte was acting very naughty in the church nursery, and the minister's wife was trying to control her.

"Charlotte darling," the lady began, "do you know that when I was a little girl, I had to do what the grown people told me to do? And when my mother was a little girl, she had to do what the grown people told her to do. And when my grandmother was a little girl, *she* had to do what the grown people told her to do."

"Good grief!" murmured Charlotte. "I wondered who ever started this silly business!"

Little Robin was having one of her bad days. To punish her, Mother made her go and stay in her room, just before a favorite children's television program came on in the family den. "Now when you say your prayers," stern Mother suggested, "ask God to make you a good girl tomorrow."

"Why," demanded Robin. "What's on tomorrow?"

+

Barry Randall had snuck into his Mom's pantry and cut a huge chunk of his Mom's newly-made cake, which she had planned to take to the church bazaar.

"Shame!" she looked hard at him. "Doesn't your conscience bother you, snitching cake this way?"

"No ma'am," said he. "It's devil's food."

+

"You know what one duck said to the other?" the sassy lad asked the plump wife of the minister, when she came to visit. Of course she said, "no." "It said, 'Oh stop walking like a woman wearing slacks!'"

+

A little boy and a little girl were in the back yard. Roger had eaten his apple, but Margie hadn't eaten hers. "Let's play Adam and Eve," suggested Roger.

"How?" asked Margie.

"Well," explained Roger, "you tempt me to eat your apple, and I'll give in."

+

Little Miss Louise was very much interested in the devil, especially about where he lived and all that; his *underground* regions seemed to be fascinating.

One night after finishing her bath, she pulled the drain plug and said to her minister-daddy, "Now the devil can take a bath!"

+

The minister's wife had to be away from home, on the very night that the bishop was a dinner guest. But eight-year-old Jeannie sat herself in mother's chair and pretended to be hostess.

The bishop beheld her with glee, and played up to her. "So you are the mother, tonight, hmmm. Well tell me, mother, where in the Bible could I find out about David and Goliath?"

He didn't discombobulate Mother Jeannie one bit. She replied with great solemnity, "I'm busy. Ask your father."

+

The preacher had called at their home, and before dinner was chatting with thirteen-year-old-and-very-sophisticated Gloria. She mentioned that one of her older girl friends had received a friendship ring from a boy, and that a slightly older friend had received an engagement ring.

This girl talk amused the minister, but he strung along. "Ah, yes. And just what is the difference between a friendship ring and an engagement ring?"

"Oh," said Gloria, as if he were indeed naive, "once you are engaged, the friendship is over."

It was the second Sunday after Christmas. The Reverend Bill Vogel spoke to small parishioner Johnny Blake in the church patio, "And did your family go out of town after Christmas, John?"

"Naw, we stayed home. But I got a good paying job, though."

"A job? How nice! What were you doing?"

"My dad pays me fifty cents a week not to play my new drums."

+

Seems the preacher had reprimanded two small boys for breaking a window in the church library. "Do you know what the truth means?" he demanded of one lad.

"Yeah," said the boy. "It means which one of us did it."

+

This mother was completely exasperated; her six-year-old Charlie Bill had been on a tear for days, and she had been unable to cope with him. Come Sunday, he even misbehaved badly in the Sunday School and church halls.

"You are a veritable tyrant!" the distraught mother exclaimed.

Charlie Bill looked interested. "What's that?"

"A tyrant?" Mom snapped. "That's a monster with horns and a tail. Like the devil has."

"Don't be crazy," the boy said. "That's a bull."

+

"Who can tell us," asked the Sunday School teacher, "the name of the first man and the first woman?"

Replied the little boy, "Adam and Evil."

5

POLISHED HALOS

Babies are angels whose wings grow shorter as their legs grow longer. Some of them grow up to be twelve-year-old angels-in-ignorance. Such as young Willie Walter Winniger of Houston, Texas, who joined the pastor's special class in preparation for church membership. That day, the pastor opened his Bible and said, "Now young folk, we will all read a chapter in unison."

Bright Willie Walt spoke right up, "Is that book in the Old or the New Testament?"

+

A visiting preacher was speaking to a group of boys. He asked each one why he attended church regularly. Several routine and expected answers were heard, then he came to the minister's son. That boy thought seriously for a moment and replied, "I guess it just sort of runs in our family."

+

Hundreds of preachers had gathered in the big Los Angeles hotel for a convention. A reporter asked the twelve-year-old elevator boy what he thought of them. "They come here," said he, "with a ten-dollar bill in one pocket and the Ten Commandments in the other, and they won't break either one."

The adult members of the family had been dithering for days, enjoying all the excitement of the approaching nuptials. Now they had put on their best clothes and started off to church for the wedding itself.

"What's a wedding?" demanded four-year-old Horatio.

His very sophisticated seven-year-old sister answered. "You are much-too-young to understand. But a wedding is something between school and a funeral."

+

 This small lad had a grandmother who had just died, so he wrote and posted this important letter: "Dear Angels. We have sent Grandma to you. Please give her a harp or a violin to play, because she is short-winded and can not blow a trumpet. But save me a trumpet, because I like it best. I hope you are all well. Jimmy."

+

The preacher was smiling fatuously at the assembled children. "All of you who want to go to heaven, please raise your hands."

Everybody's hand shot up except sweet little Ellen's.

"Don't you want to go to Heaven, Ellen?" the minister asked.

"Yeth thir," Ellen lisped eagerly, "but I'd rather go tomorrow because Mommy is having ice cream for dethert today."

+

Sweet little Periwinkle Jones (which just might
be the cutest name a girl child can have!) was disturbed by nature's noises and actions just after
bedtime. Mommy came in to comfort her, "Oh,
darling, don't be afraid. A thunderstorm is only the
sound of the angels making their beds."

It was a bit far fetched, but Periwinkle swallowed it. Next morning, though, she reported,
"Mommy, I didn't mind the noise when the angels
made their beds, but I was unhappy when they
kept turning the lights on and off."

The very young and correct young lady was being registered for pre-school. She had watched the procedure with other children, and when her turn came she spoke right out, "I am Ruth Elizabeth Evans, and I am half Welsh and half Protestant."

+

The preacher asked some teen-agers for a definition, and got it. One girl said, "When adults act like children, they are silly; when children act like adults, they are delinquents."

+

The preacher and a group of his small parishioners were touring the zoo, and came onto a strange bird. The preacher eyed it and wondered aloud, "Whatever is that?"

"It's an apteryx," said one bright lad.

"Hm-m-m-m-m," mused the minister, stroking his chin and staring. "Now that's not my idea of an apteryx."

"Maybe not," replied the boy, "But it's God's idea of an apteryx."

+

At the smiling minister's insistence, little Percival was telling him of his life's ambition — "When I grow up I shall be a lion tamer. I will walk right into the cages with fierce tigers and leopards and lions, then I shall . . ."

"Oh, ho," the preacher interrupted, "but won't you be afraid in that cage with so many ferocious animals snarling at you?"

"Oh, I won't be alone," Percival reassured him, "I'll have my mother with me."

Five-year-old Roscoe, like the cartooned Dennis, was having to sit in the corner because of naughtiness. He had been told to ask God's forgiveness, which he dutifully did. Then after a short pause he said to his mother, "I just can't help it if I'm not perfect. I guess I've heard of only one perfect boy anyhow."

Mother grasped this as excellent opportunity to develop a moral lesson; obviously her little son's thoughts had turned to the boy Jesus. She spoke softly, "And who was He, darling?"

The lad stymied her. "It was Daddy, when he was a boy."

+

The preacher, being too erudite at Vacation Bible School, ranged afar in his testing of the twelve-year-olds. "What," asked he, "is relative humidity?"

One boy had an immediate answer — "It happens when you hold your baby brother on your lap."

+

The church Session had gathered at the home of the minister, twelve dignified and dedicated gentlemen. The meeting opened with a prayer. The evening's business was about to begin, when the preacher's very small and sweet daughter rushed in, struggling with the back button of her pajamas.

"Daddy," she broke up the meeting, "will you please open my bathroom door?"

+

Repentance? It was defined best and for all of us for all time by a little girl, when she said, "It means to be sorry enough to quit."

This little girl answered a question in Vacation Bible School thus, "The Bible says go ye into all the world and preach the gossip," Of course, millions of us obey that interpretation.

+

First service was at 9:30 o'clock, but this Sunday morning young Jerry Derryberrry got to church at 8. Lo, the minister was alone in the big sanctuary, standing at his pulpit, going at it full force.

"How come that?" Jerry asked the minister's small son.

"Oh," replied he, "Dad always practices what he preaches."

+

A guest was coming to dinner, and he was crippled. Mother warned little Oswald not to mention the guest's amputated leg.

"No ma'am, I won't," he promised. Then his halo shone even brighter when he added, "And when I get to heaven, I won't say anything to John the Baptist about his head, either."

+

The John Eakin home in Kingsville, Ohio, had a custom that all of us could and should emulate; the parents maintained a table as a worship center in the home, with candles and a Bible on it.

But you know how careless we all are at times. So it was right and proper when three-year-old Sonny Eakin was discovered leaving that room with his arms full of books, magazines, pencils, gloves and such.

"Can't have all this mess on God's table," he muttered, unconsciously shaming the older folk.

+

6

QUESTIONABLE HALOS

In the municipal park, an elderly woman was sitting in the shade knitting, near the public swimming pool. A small boy rather diffidently approached her, "Ma'am, do you go to Sunday School?"

"Why, yes, I do," she smiled down at him. "Every Sunday."

"And to church, too?"

"Dear me, yes!" her interest was growing.

"And do you say your prayers every night?"

"Every night, sometimes oftener."

"Okay, then," the lad held out a hand, "I guess it's safe for me to leave these three pennies with you while I go in swimming."

+

It is important, said the preacher to his group of small boys, that we be kind to dumb animals. Of course it is. The lads all agreed. So the good man asked them to recount instances when they had actually defended some poor beast. Butch Hale held up a hand.

"Sir, only last Saturday I beat up the boy next door because he kicked my dog."

+

The Reverend Bill Vogal may really be the smartest man in the world — a lot of his parishioners often think so. One day in the church study, this very humble man had a telephone call from his home.

"Hello," said a very sweet six-year-old voice. "Who is this please?"

He recognized his daughter, grinned, and replied in disguised voice, "This is the smartest man in the world."

Little daughter remained polite. "Pardon me, sir, I have the wrong number."

+

The head usher of a church encountered two small boys on the street and recognized one of them. "Good morning, Robert."

"Who was that?" Robert's friend asked.

"Oh, he's one of the waiters at our church."

+

Gallantry is not to be ignored, even among the very young. It happened that seven-year-old Walter was an admirer of seven-year-old Louise, and they sat together in a row of children in big church this morning. The time came when the collection plate was approaching. Every child got out a coin — except Louise.

"Don't you have any money?" whispered Walter.

"No," she whispered back, embarrassed.

Well, a man has to rise to such occasions, but Walt had only the one nickel.

"Here, take mine," he whispered hurriedly. "It will pay for you, and I will hide under the seat."

In May's Landing, New Jersey, Mrs. David Cope showed her five-year-old son Davey a picture of parents holding a baby at the church baptismal font. She asked if he know what was about to happen to the baby.

"Oh sure," Davey replied. "The baby is going to be hypnotized."

Four-year-old Suzette came to church early with her parents who had a duty there. Suzy wandered around and soon approached an assistant pastor. "Where is the coke machine?" she demanded.

"Oh, I'm afraid our church has no coke machine," said he.

"Then where is the candy machine?" Suzy continued.

"Candy machine?" the preacher was astonished anew. "We don't have a candy machine, either."

"Well for heaven's sake, then," Suzy was exasperated, "why did mother give me this dime?"

 The Reverend Charles C. Miller, Jr., reported on a lack of understanding in his class of boys at Jacksonville, Texas. Church services had long been over, the sanctuary was virtually empty. But, the collection plates were still down there on the altar rail, unemptied.

"Are you *sure* God will come down and get that money?" one worried.

+

Four-year-old Dennis knew all about weddings; he had seen them pictured in magazines. He was very much impressed by the recent wedding of his Aunt Patty, up in Jackson, Michigan. One day, he said to his grandmother, Henrietta Steffen, "I wish my mommy and daddy were married."

Aghast, Grandma said, "Why they *are*!"

Wise Denny shook his head, "Why wasn't I invited?"

"Do cows and bees go to heaven?" very young Mirielle asked. Of course mother said "no." "Then," reasoned the child, "all that milk and honey the preacher said was up there, must be canned stuff."

+

Now here is one with a painful moral for all of us.

Very small Johnny developed a penchant for doing and saying unkind things. So his father said, "For every mistake like that, son, we will drive a nail into the front gate post. But for every kindness you show, we will pull out a nail. Okay?"

Johnny agreed. But unfortunately, the post was soon bristling with nails.

Johnny had a long talk about it with his kindly minister, and things began to improve; John was maturing, gaining self-control. After about a month, "Hey there, Son!" the proud father beamed now at his son. "Congratulations. There's not one nail left in the post."

John looked at it with a new wistfulness and said, "No, sir. But the scars remain."

+

Mrs. Link also helped a family that had been in critical need. As she finally left this home, a small girl there said, "Thank you very much, Mrs. Link. God bless you, and may you have life as long as you live."

(Don't belittle that blessing! Too many of us don't have life as we live, we merely have existence.)

+

This mother yelled at her energetic small son, "Junior, what are you doing out there?"

Junior answered truthfully — "Nothing worth mentioning. What with you and Jesus watching me all the time, I am afraid to do much."

+

In a remote country village in England a new mailbox had been set up. The village children were much interested.

"I think it belongs to the doctor or the squire," one said.

"No," said another, "Can't you see it's by the church? So it must be the minister's".

"Can't be," replied the first very smart lad. "The sign on it says 'No Collection On Sundays.'"

+

Consider this devastating commentary —

At a Church in St. Paul, Minnesota, two four year olds were sitting together, when the choir processional began. The sopranos and altos in their robes led the way. Behind them marched the tall and stately basses, baritones and tenors. The music came to a sudden pause.

In the silence, one lad piped out, "Which one of those men is God?"

The startled congregation heard a most disturbing answer from the other boy, and some wondered if it could be true: "Neither one of them. God doesn't come to our church."

+

7

UTTER ADULT EXASPERATION

(By the time our children are old enough not to say or do anything in public to disgrace us, they have reached an age when the things we say and do embarrass them.)

The Reverend Aaron Powers, who is the very essence of kindness, said to his six-year-old Willie, "Son, run over and ask how old Mrs. Smithers is this afternoon."

Willie came back and reported, "She said it was none of your business."

The pastor was appalled. "But she has been very ill! Whatever did you say to her, son?"

"Just what you told me to," replied Willie. "I asked her how old she was."

+

The encyclopedia salesman had called at the home. Mother tried to brush him off, but six-year-old Pete seemed interested and the salesman took courage from that.

"This set of books," said he, "will educate your son, ma'am. It will answer every question he can ever ask." He beamed down at Pete. "Go ahead, sonny, ask me a question, any question. Then I will show your mother how easy it is to find the answer in one of these books."

Pete was willing to cooperate. He gave serious thought to it for a moment, then asked, "What kind of car does God drive?"

+

Young Ned Preston was in summer camp, but kept insisting that he had to be back home by Saturday noon, nearly 100 miles away. Finally the camp director gave in, and personally drove Ned all the way back. As they neared town, Ned said, "Just drop me off at the bus station, please."

"The bus station?" The director was surprised. "But I thought you were so anxious to get home, to see your parents. Why the bus station?"

"No," said Ned. "I want to go to another camp and the bus for it leaves at noon."

+

Here we have another one of those uninhibited modern-generation kids who speak out boldly. He had been taken into big church for the first time, and naturally was interested in all the rituals and routines there. The time came for the buxom soprano to stand up and sing her solo. The choir director also stood near her with his baton, to lead the choir behind her in certain passages of the anthem. The organ began, the baton lifted and began fanning the air vigorously, the soprano started on high C and soared on upward.

Little Oswald's view from back in the 17th row of pews was somewhat obscured, but he was fascinated.

"Hey Mom," he asked, "why is that man hitting that lady with that stick?"

"Sh-h-h, be quiet. He's not hitting her with a stick."

"Then," asked Oswald, "what's she hollerin' so loud for?"

Church was over, and the steeple people were fraternizing over coffee in the patio, when around the corner lickety-split ran little Roscoe Stanford, age nine, and he was crying.

"Here, here, Roscoe my lad," said the kindly Reverend Dr. Hall. "What is the matter? You have bruises and look beat."

"Well s-sir," Roscoe began, "I challenged Billy Norman to a duel, and gave him choice of weapons." Roscoe paused to wail louder for a moment, then added. "But I n-never thought he would c-choose his sister!"

+

The church folk were about to break ground for a big new sanctuary. There stood five pastors and twelve deacons, all holding shovels, ready for the symbolic service. Finally each one turned about a teacup full of earth. Mostly, the service was one of prayer and singing.

Enroute home, the minister's little daughter was asked how she liked the ceremony.

"It was terrible," said she. "So many people, and so little work!"

+

Four-year-old Linda told her mother, "I have almost forgotten how to fly through the air."

Mother looked serious, because the preacher had called and was sitting in the parlor with them. "Now Linda dear," she purred. "Remember what you learned in Sunday School. You mustn't tell lies. You know that you never flew through the air."

"But Mama, you yourself told me that the stork brought me here."

This missionary had a captive audience when he came back to America after years abroad. Here was his chance to justify all his work and perhaps get bigger appropriations for further endeavor. He spoke at great length. He showed motion pictures. He showed slides. He prayed. He was very emotional with it all, pointing up the need for more missionaries to help him.

At the end, he saw a small boy waiting to speak with him. Perhaps he had a convert here, who would grow up into the Good Work.

"I can guess what you want to say to me," he beamed at the lad. "I feel sure that you want to be a missionary some day. Right?"

"Oh, no, sir," said the wide-eyed boy. "I was just wondering if you have any foreign stamps?"

+

Even if you have heard it before, this — the finest of all the kid stories is worth repeating.

The fashionable pastor of the fashionable First Fifth Avenue Ecumenical Cathedral had been invited to the million-dollar home of the fashionable Honorable and Madame Fitzmaurice Fitzwilliam III. They and other elegantly attired guests were in the elegant drawing room about 9 p.m., when they heard the patter of tiny feet and the poetic whisperings of tiny voices at the head of the plushly carpeted stairs.

"Sh-h-h-," admonished Madame Fitzwilliam, smiling at her guests, "the children are coming down for us to hear their goodnight prayers."

The group became silent, except that the pompous pastor there murmured, "So sweet! So sentimental!"

The dramatic silence held them until beautiful little Mirielle Marie Fitzwilliam, clad in her expensive little silk nightie, paused on the bottom step there and almost shouted her news —

"Mother, Moth-er, Larry found a bedbug!"

+

The aging parson, dutifully trudging around town making calls at the homes of his people, came to a poor apartment building. Studying his little notebook, he nodded; this had to be the right address. There on the sidewalk stood some men talking. Nearby was a sleepy-looking small boy. He spoke to the boy.

"Sonny, does Mr. Keating live in this building?"

"Yep."

"Where?"

"Away up high."

The good minister thought to be kind. "Well, would you show me to his door if I gave you a dime?"

"Yep. Come on."

They climbed six long flights of rickety stairs. The parson was pooped, and had to stop to catch his breath. Oh! how his rheumatic leg ached! Naturally he then rang Mr. Keating's doorbell, hoping for a chair to sit upon soon. But no one answered.

"Mr. Keating doesn't seem to be at home," he lamented at last.

"Nope," agreed the boy "That was him standing on the doorstep just as we came in the building."

+

*Very young Montmorency had returned home.
"Mother," said he, "On the way to Sunday School
I met our new preacher, and he asked me if I ever
played marbles on Sunday."*

"And what did you say to that, dear?"

*"Well, I really wanted to play, but I remained
strong like you told me to. I just said 'Get thee
behind me, Satan,' then ran off and left him."*

+

The preacher's little boy was growing, and becoming more troublesome than ever. Papa had an
unpleasant session with him one afternoon, came
back into the living room, and sighed to Mrs.
Preacher, "He is getting too big to spank, and too
smart to out-argue. I will be grateful when he falls
in love, so that some young girl can take him down
a notch or two."

+

"Go bring me the broom from the basement
closet," Mother told five-year-old Timmy.

He went down there, opened the door but
quickly closed it and rushed back to tell Mother it
was as dark as pitch in there, hence dangerous.

"Oh no, Darling, do not be afraid. God is everywhere, God will take care of you always."

"He's even in that closet?"

"Of course."

None too sure, Tim went back, opened the door
a crack, and said, "God, please hand me the
broom."

+

The wedding was over, the people, including small guest John Joe Davis, were in the reception hall. John Joe eyed the blushing bride, then exasperated his parents as well as embarrassed them. He said, "Hey, you don't look tired out, like I thought you would."

"Really, John Joe?" replied the sweet bride. "Why should I look so tired?"

"Well, Mom said you had been running after Mr. Smith for months."

It is nice to be thoughtful of others, especially in our prayers. Six-year-old Tom Paul Hughs once was overheard praying, "Please, God, take care of my little brother Georgie, until he gets big enough to fight."

+

Also there was the preacher who had a captive audience of kids before him, and he preached on, and on, and on, and on endlessly. Finally one child piped out, "He's running down, he needs a new needle."

+

Finally, here is still another child classic, too good not to record, especially since new-generation readers may not have encountered this bit of pastoral guidance:

"Liars never go to heaven, Johnny," the preacher warned his son.

The boy considered that. "Did my grandfather ever tell a lie?"

"Why yes, I suppose so." (after all, nobody's perfect, eh?)

"Did Mother?"

"Yes, no doubt." He could remember some moments . . .!

"Did you? And Grandmother? And Aunt Emma?"

"Why, why, I suppose we all have, a time or two." The matter was becoming involved even for a pastor. He must now explain Christ's forgiveness to the boy.

Johnny shook his head sadly and walked off, saying, "It must get awful lonesome up in heaven, with nobody there but George Washington and God."

8

SAINTS IN SUNDAY SCHOOL

In Wilkesboro, North Carolina, the late Miss Essie Erwin was teaching her Sunday School class about "Reaping The Tares." She asked if any child could give the subject for the day, and up shot a hand, frantically waving. "Yes," said this child, "the subject today is ripping and tearing."

+

Johnny Barry seemed delighted with his first visit to Sunday School, and returned with eagerness next Sunday. But the following week, his mother was nonplussed when he refused, to the point of hysteria, when she tried to send him for a third class. Finally she called the teacher and asked, "Could you have said anything to upset him or frighten him?"

"No, certainly not," teacher replied. "I was so glad to see him coming regularly, that I told him I would put him in the Register."

+

"Why," asked this Sunday School teacher of her class, "would it be sinful to cut off the tail of a cat?"

Little Ricky Turek had what might be called a right answer, "Because, ma'am, the Bible says what God has joined together, let no man put asunder."

It was examination day in Sunday School, and a lot of questions had been asked. Here are some of the juvenile answers as turned in on the papers:

Saints are dead clergymen.

The chief end of man is the end with the head on.

The father of the cow kept at the Vatican to supply the Pope with milk was called the Papal Bull.

Only lady choir members sing alto, which is a low form of music.

King Solomon's robes were trimmed with vermin.

A post-mortem means you shouldn't have died yet.

A vacuum is a large empty space where the Pope lives.

Fiction are books in the church library which are fixed to the shelves and cannot be removed.

The Red Sea and the Mediterranean Sea are connected by the Sewage Canal.

+

This was a very fancy Sunday School dinner. Little Randy tried oysters for the first time. Presently they were passed again, but he murmured "No thank you, I don't know what to do with the ones I've got now."

+

In Woods Memorial Presbyterian Church at Severna Park, Maryland, Mrs. Helen Mills asked her Sunday School class if they knew what Lent was.

Up shot several small hands, and one girl got the nod. "It's the white stuff," said she, "that gets on clothes in the washing machine."

"No," another corrected instantly, "it's the fuzzy stuff under my granddaddy's bed at home."

The Sunday School had a special party to honor young Robert Harris, who had rescued a friend when he dropped through thin ice.

"Now tell us," said the S.S. Superintendent, hoping to build a moral, "just what motivated you, Bobby? Why did you bravely rush out there on that dangerous lake to rescue your friend?"

"Had to," declared Bobby, very honestly. "He was wearing my skates."

+

Teacher asked her class, "What does the Bible mean when it says Jesus healed many divers diseases?"

Little Betty Lou knew the answer instantly. "It means He healed people sick from swimming."

+

Ebullient young David reported at home that Sunday School teacher asked him not to return because he was a "scurvy elephant."

Naturally, mother investigated that. What David had really been told was that he was a "disturbing element."

+

Pretty Miss Clieo Davis, a beloved Sunday School teacher, got on the town bus one Wednesday. Seeing a face that appeared familiar, she smiled and said, "Why hello, Mr. Jones."

When he gave no answering sign of recognition, she blushed and apologized, "Do forgive me. I thought you were the father of one of my children."

In Westminster, California, three-year-old Michael VanderSchaaf had attended several neighborhood parties in the past few weeks, and was delighted with them, especially with the cakes and ice cream. Soon he was introduced to Sunday School, and after his first session there his mother asked how he had liked it.

"I didn't," said the disgruntled boy. "Nothing to eat."

+

Even if you don't understand this one, the good folk in the anthracite coal area of Pennsylvania will. In a Wilkesbarre Sunday School, reports Herbert Bircher, the teacher asked one of the youngsters, "Where was Christ born?"

Instantly one lad answered, "Allentown."

"No, my dear," she corrected gently, "Christ was born in Bethlehem."

"Well," said the youngster, "I knew it was some place in the Lehigh Valley here."

+

"Who was Peter?" teacher asked the very young Sunday Schoolers.

One little girl yelped, "Peter was a pumpkin eater!"

+

Sophisticated Sonny, age four, returned home from Sunday School, and his mother (who should have been there with him) fatuously asked, "And how was Sunday School today, darling?"

Her very sober darling shrugged and replied, "Not so good. That man Daniel, he's in the den with the lions again."

+

About that lion's den again — it seems that teacher had shown her class pictures of the martyrs actually in the den with the ferocious beasts. There were many lions, but only four martyrs.

"It looks like," began young, Joe Bob Wilson, "there is a shortage. Those young lions in the back will be lucky if they get a single bite."

You know how these advertising slogans go; how they make indelible impact on our minds. In Denver, Mrs. C. John Dikovics asked her Sunday School class of three-year-olds how God's sunshine helps to grow. But one sharp kid piped up, "Oxydol beats the sunshine!"

+

With what weapon did Samson slay a thousand Philistines? "Undoubtedly," said one small boy in Sunday School "With the ax of the Apostles."

+

Mrs. Rosemary Detwiler had been teaching this class of rather wild lads for weeks, and patience was wearing thin, especially with restless young Rocky Malone. Each week he was in his seat, squirming, whispering, talking out of turn, showing off, losing his offering nickel.

One Sunday he suddenly clapped his hand over his mouth and gasped.

Mrs. Detwiler paused and resignedly asked, "What is it now, Rocky."

"I-I swallowed my nickel!"

She refused to panic. She merely shrugged and resumed the lesson after saying, "Well there's one good thing about it. For once, you know where it is."

+

Five-year-old Jennifer Henderson in Dallas came home from her Sunday School, and her papa asked what the teacher had talked about.

Said sweet Jennifer, "Oh, she talked about the goodest American."

It took papa a week to learn that the subject had really been on the Good Samaritan."

In Berkshire, New York, Mildred Brown's sister was teaching her primary class about Joseph. "What was it that Joseph's father gave him?" she asked.

Lispy Lisbeth raised her hand and replied, "A bright red thweater!"

+

State pride and loyalty can be many-splendored. A Sunday School teacher in Los Angeles was briefing her class about the hardships of the Puritans on the East Coast, telling how they had to worship amid untold hardships, live in crude homes, suffer intense cold and heavy rains, all that. "Many were destined to perish that first winter," she lamented, then paused for any reaction her pupils might have.

Bright young Phillip had one, "Why didn't they come to California?"

+

"When do friends drop in most often?" teacher asked, after her moralizings on fellowship and friendship and stuff like that there.

Young Tod James had an accurate answer, "When the television is broken and the refrigerator is empty."

+

Said the teacher, "Now boys and girls, what kind of children go to heaven?"

Oh, of course, sir, you know the answer. Or do you? Could you have been as accurate as little Butch Bancroft?

Replied Butch, "I know, teacher. Dead ones."

In Morrisville, Pennsylvania, Mrs. Jean Harshberger had been gently lecturing her Sunday School class on the manner in which Jesus chose a disciple. Finally she asked the group of seven-year-olds if they really knew what a disciple was.

One boy seemed to be sure he knew, "Well, it's just about like a side-kick."

(Which, come to think of it, wasn't too bad a definition.)

+

In this Sunday School the several teachers took turns addressing the assembly. Most of them of course tried dutifully to point up the lesson, always saying at the end, "And now the moral of this story is. . . ."

One Sunday pretty Miss Ann Niewold did an extra-fine job. The kids were delighted. They asked if she could do the speaking every Sunday. The superintendent asked "why?"

"Because," said they in unison, "Miss Ann hasn't any morals."

+

F. M. Reed in Rochester, New York, reports on a seven-year-old boy who went to Sunday School. Upon his return home, his family asked him what he had learned.

His reply was emphatic. "I learned to love God, sit down, SIT DOWN, SIT DOWN!"

+

This sweet little girl was in error, let us hope, when she wrote on her Sunday School examination paper, "We Presbyterians are God's frozen people."

Then there was little Jean. As always, as they reached the door of their church, Mother opened her purse and handed Jean a dime for Sunday School.

But Jeannie grew to the mature age of five, so this Sunday at the church door she looked questioningly into the older eyes and asked, "Mommy, how many more years do I have to pay to get into Sunday School?"

Jimmy Schuman, son of the local mortician, listened with interest to the Sunday School lesson about the death of Joseph. "Any questions?" teacher asked.

"Yes," said Jim at once, "who got the funeral?"

+

At home for Sunday dinner, the head of the house asked, "Well, what did you learn in Sunday School today, Junior?"

Ten-year-old Junior Jones looked thoughtful, then replied, "Well, our teacher told us about Moses."

"What about Moses?"

"Well, God sent him behind the enemy lines to rescue the Israelites. Down in Egypt, he had them meet him at midnight to slip out of town. Soon they came to the Red Sea and couldn't get across. Moses called for engineers to build a pontoon bridge. After they had all crossed, they looked back and saw the Egyptian tanks coming."

Mother tried to interrupt, but Junior plunged on.

"Right quick, Moses picked up his walkie-talkie and radioed his headquarters to send bombers to blow up the bridge that him and the Israelites had just crossed over. WHAM! ... BOOM! ... Down came the bombs from the B-52s. They blew up the bridge and saved the Israelites."

"Junior!" Mother was appalled. "You know that your Sunday School teacher didn't tell the story that way!"

Junior shrugged. "No, not exactly," replied her young angel of the space age. "But if I told it just like she did, you would never believe it."

9

PITY THE POOR TEACHER

Pity and sympathy do indeed belong to Mrs. Preston Battle of Memphis, according to reports from the Presbyterian Day School there.

It seems that her son, Preston, Jr., won a medal because he had read no less than 405 books during the session — an all-time record for the pupils there. Imagine it — 405 books! What's more, the lad had read them all aloud, too, in order to get the credit.

So at commencement program, Preston Jr. naturally was called to the rostrum to receive a medal and honors for his achievement.

But the history-making aspect came when Mrs. Battle herself was called up there and awarded a medal. Why?

For listening — what else!

+

Young Monty was late for Sunday School. Of course, the teacher asked for an explanation.

"I was going fishing," Monty explained, "but Dad wouldn't let me."

"Of course not," she replied. "You should be proud of him."

"Yes'm," agreed forlorn looking Monty. "He said there wasn't enough bait for both of us."

+

The teacher was conscientious; she had prayed and worked and strived to get her good moral points across to the Sunday School lads and lassies. Today, she was especially concerned with the story of Jonah and the whale, which is somewhat hard for anybody to understand fully. She talked, explained, and did her best. Then she asked, "Now does everybody know what this story teaches us?"

"Sure," declared seven-year-old Matthew. "It teaches us that you can't keep a good man down."

+

The good teacher said, "Yes, Lot was duly warned. He was told to take his wife and flee out of the city, but she stopped to look back and was turned into a pillar of salt."

She paused for that dramatic fact to sink in. Presently one small lad asked, "Teacher, what became of the flea?"

+

This may be the all-time favorite story about children in Sunday School.

"What must we do before we can obtain forgiveness for sin?" teacher asked the class.

Johnny Smith gave an obvious answer, "We must sin."

+

The pastor encountered a little boy in the patio after first service this Sunday morning and asked him, "Do you love to attend Sunday School, Harold?"

"Oh, yes, sir."

"And what did you learn this morning?"

"The date for the picnic."

"Who led the Israelites out of Egypt?" the teacher in San Francisco asked her class.

No answer came, so she finally pointed to a big-eyed lad in the rear of the room and asked him.

"Please ma'am, it wasn't me," he declared timidly. "We just moved to California last week; we came from Iowa."

Spring had sprung, June was in tune with the moon over the lagoon, all that. So when Sunday School teacher asked her class of junior high school girls to name a favorite hymn, dreamy-eyed Valerie instantly said, "Rick Harris, the baseball captain."

+

The formally dressed minister came in and told the Sunday School class a long story, then concluded, "Does anyone have a question?"
One lad held up a hand.
"Yes, William?"
"Sir, how do you get into your collar?"

Grandmother was trying to furnish what is known as child guidance. "Very often," said she to her six-year-old Sharon Gail, "Sunday School will have some very naughty boys in it, who act impudent and tease one another and disturb the class, and sometimes little girls smile at them. Now I hope my sweet granddaughter never behaves in such fashion."

"No, never, Grandmother," Sharie assured her earnestly. "I stick my tongue out at them."

+

Miss Wendy Lee, age six, was walking with her Daddy. She spoke to a small boy who passed them.

"Who was that?" Daddy asked.

"Roger. He's in my Sunday School class."

"Roger who? What is his last name?" Daddy insisted.

"His whole name is Roger Sitdown. That's what the teacher calls him."

Maurice didn't play much football or baseball, perhaps because he wore glasses; but he had his status in other competitions. One day the Sunday School teacher asked her class, "When Lot's wife looked back contrary to God's orders, what happened to her?"

True, some lesser brain might have answered correctly also. But Maurice stood up first and elucidated, "She was deplorably transmuted into choride of sodium."

Here's another old favorite from the world of small fry.

"My young friend," asked the pastor, "do you know the parables?"

"Yes, sir," replied Johnny. "We study them in Sunday School."

"Fine, fine. And which one do you like the best?"

"I like the one where everybody loafs and fishes."

+

Barbara, aged four, came home from Sunday School and asked, "Mommy, does God stand on His head to make the sun shine?"

Mother was astonished. "No, Dear. Whatever gave you such an idea?"

"Well they gave us this picture card showing God, and He has this shiny ring around his head. Isn't that the sun?"

+

In class the small children were singing *Jesus wants me for a sunbeam.* Beverly piped out, "What's a sunbeam?"

Before teacher could intervene, Master Butch Hale replied, "Dopey, it's a waffle iron!"

+

Very young Erin O'Reilly attended Sunday School for the first time, and her Irish energies found new outlet there. When her mother called for her and asked, "How did you like it, darling?" Erin said it was fine.

"And what did the teacher tell you?" mother pursued.

Replied Erin, "To be quiet."

The Sunday School teacher was finally forced to report on tough little Roscoe to his mother.

"Shame on you, son," Mom chided. "When you first started to Sunday School, you were so nice all the time. Now teacher says you are the rowdiest, noisiest one there!"

Roscoe shrugged. "I just learned that they don't have no time off for good behavior in that joint."

+

The little girl was overheard telling her friend how Sunday School class was begun each week. "We stand up," said she, "and put our hands over our hearts to see if we are still alive."

+

Of course you know why Solomon was the wisest man in the world. Little Marian learned why in Sunday School, and told the class when teacher asked her, "It was because he had so many wives to advise him."

+

"The Bible lesson today," began the Sunday School teacher, "is about the strongest man who ever lived. He could do almost anything. Now can anybody tell me his name? It begins with an S."

Instantly the whole class spoke out, *"Superman!"*

+

The Sunday School teacher had caught William in, shall we say, a slight prevarication. Severely she demanded, "Willie, do you know what happens to liars when they die?"

"Yes, ma'am," replied this innocent. "They lie still."

This teacher asked her class if they wished to go to heaven, and all members, except one boy, raised their hands.

"You don't want to go to heaven, Jerry?" she asked.

"Yes, ma'am, " replied Jerry, "but my mother told me to come straight home as soon as Sunday School was over today."

+

The probing preacher asked an attorney's little son in Sunday School, "My boy, do you know where wicked men eventually go?"

"Sure," replied the lad. "They practice law in town for a few years, then they go to the state legislature."

+

Graduation time had come, and the children were being registered in new Sunday School classes. "What is your name, little man?" one teacher fatuously asked.

"Jule."

"Do not use a nickname. I will write it correctly in the records, Julius. Now, next boy, what is your name?"

Said the second lad, "Billious, ma'am."

+

Very young pastor, Rev. Roy Shepler, in Phoenix was called on suddenly to go speak to a Sunday School class of ten-year-olds. Of course he had nothing prepared, so to give himself time to think, he asked, "Well, young people, what shall I talk about?"

Miss Chris Green, who had memorized several speeches in school, spoke out, "What do you know?"

The Sunday School teacher had a class of recalcitrant little reprobates and stinkers — no, no, in this modern age we must call them sweet little misunderstood under- achievers. Anyhow, one of the darlings overstepped his psyche or something, and teacher had to remonstrate, "Harold, why did you kick Marcia in the stomach?"

"I couldn't help it," wailed five-year-old Harold. "She turned around too fast."

+

This Sunday School believed in dramatizing Bible morals with stories that could have specific modern application. So the teacher said to the class of young boys, "Forgiveness is always a virtue. Could you, for example, forgive another boy if he had hit you with his fist?"

The class gave serious thought to so grave a matter, and finally one smallish lad said, "Yes sir, I could if he was bigger than me."

+

Salty old wives are not necessarily the best kind, although some men do have to put up with them.

"What happened to Lot's wife when she looked back?" the preacher asked the Sunday School class on test day.

"She turned to salt," one boy recited.

"Correct," nodded the minister. "And what did Lot do then?"

After a short pause to think, the boy added, "Well, I guess he looked around for a fresh wife."

+

"If the pretty angels that talked to Jacob all had wings," began sharp-minded little Robin O'Reilly in her Sunday School class, "why did they have to climb up and down a ladder?"

(Will some reader please mail in a reasonable answer?)

+

"Why do bells ring at Christmas?" this sentimental, benevolent Sunday School teacher asked her class of hotshot kids.

All right, why do they? . . . Can you give correct answer? Young Johnny Mehagian could, and he spoke up instantly, "Because somebody is pulling the ropes."

+

The Sunday School teacher was trying to tighten down her moral lesson. "Now exactly *why*," she asked, "should we all learn to rise by our own efforts?"

Young Randy Detwiler had a correct answer, "Because there is no telling when your alarm clock will fail to ring."

+

What was the sin of the Pharisees? You don't know? Well, little Horatio did. He said it was eating camels, and he quoted authority. He insisted that his own Sunday School teacher had read aloud that the Pharisees had "strained at gnats and swallowed camels."

+

10

GROWING PAINS, DOESN'T IT?

Certainly it does. It pains the poor parents almost insufferably and drives the preacher and Sunday School teachers out of their minds. Not their growing, but the children's! The mental rebellion of our beloved kids, who begin trying to kick themselves out of the nest, and feel that they must express themselves without inhibitions. Like the boy whose father had just returned from church and now felt called on to lecture his son.

"You are getting older, Sonny," Dad began. "You must learn to be more responsible, learn to take care of yourself. Just suppose that I died suddenly, then where would you be?"

Growing young Sonny lifted his shoulders and replied, "That's not the point, Dad. The big question is, where would *you* be?"

+

"We've got a new baby at our house," sophisticated Miss Sharie Detwiler exultantly told her Sunday School teacher.

"How nice!" replied the teacher, smiling. "Is it going to stay?"

For asking so condescending a question, teacher got what she deserved. "I guess so," replied Sharie, in doubtful innocence. "He has his clothes off."

It is not only boys who cause growing pains. This pastor's wife, Dorothy, was having trouble with her sweet and pretty daughter Pamela. "Don't you realize," Mom demanded, "that if you keep on acting naughty and impudent, your children will act that way too?"

Pam beamed in triumph. "Ah ha, Mother! You just gave yourself away!"

+

But it was eight-year-old William who admitted the beaming pastor to his home. Willie had achieved a plateau of cynicism, but the good preacher saw only the boy's halo.

"I hear," the good man began, "that you have been brought a brand new baby brother by an angel. Do you want me to take you to the hospital and show you the baby, Willie?"

"Naw," scowled the lad. "Show me the angel."

+

Also we must pity the poor pastor who, while making parish calls, came onto a husky lad in a yard hammering on a girl there.

"Stop that!" cried the minister, pulling the angry boy away from the girl. "Whatever are you doing? What do you mean by hitting this little girl?"

"I got a right to hit her," countered the boy, scowling. "She cheated."

"Cheated you? How did she do that?"

"We were playing Adam and Eve," explained the boy. "She got an apple, and she was supposed to tempt me. But she didn't; she ate the apple all by herself!"

Or consider the sardonically superior student, aged twelve plus, to whom the Sunday School teacher put this question: "What was the difference between Noah's Ark and Joan of Arc?"

Of course that was a tricky question at best; teachers do have to fight back as best as they can. But this one perhaps got her come-uppance when growing Junior replied, "That's easy. Noah's Ark was made of wood, Joan of Arc was Maid of Orleans."

+

"Ah, just think of it!" exulted the poetic young Sunday School teacher, before her class of twelve-year-old boys. "A land flowing with milk and honey! I wonder what that would be like?"

She too got what she deserved. Butch Hale answered — "Sticky!"

+

Two kids were arguing. You know — my father can lick your father, mine is smarter than yours, all that.

"You know the Pacific Ocean?" one boy demanded. "Well my father bit the hole for it."

That was pretty good. But his pal paused a moment to think then said, "You've heard of the Dead Sea in the Bible? Well, my father killed it."

+

Preacher was down front, coaching the children for the big Christmas pageant, "Now let's all be so quiet you can hear a pin drop."

Silence set in. Then a voice from a rear pew shouted, "Okay, let it drop!"

The teacher at Sunday School was also a Bible Scholar (and let us pray for more of her kind). One day she saw Janie Smith's apple being avidly devoured by Ricky Turek.

"Rick," she scolded gently, "don't you realize that in stealing Janie's apple you have broken the eighth Commandment?"

Rick considered that matter while munching fast, then shrugged and ruled, "Well I guess I might as well break the eighth and enjoy the apple, as to break the tenth and only covet it."

The Sunday School teacher was trying to stress the importance of brevity in speech and in writing. So she offered a prize to the pupil among her forty who wrote the shortest, most expressive essay on two of life's problems.

The prize winning paper held just one word — "Twins."

+

"Johnny," began the Sunday School teacher, working toward a good biblical moral, "do you know what a flood is?"

Johnny was way ahead of her. "Sure, it's a river that grew too big for its bridges."

+

This was one of those "sensible" preachers, and he was lecturing the bigger boys one Sunday. "You have to grab opportunity when it comes along," said he. "An opportunist knows when he sees a chance to save his soul. William, do you understand what an opportunist is?"

"Yeah," the boy said. "It's a guy who, when he finds himself in hot water, decides he needs a bath anyway."

+

Even the small fry can pain their parents. Five-year-old Sean was caught in the bathtub one Sunday morning, sailing his toy boat. "Sean," cried mama, "haven't you been taught that the Sabbath is for praying, not for playing?"

"I'm not playing, mama," this sharp lad countered. "This is a missionary boat heading out for India."

*This was one of those churches where each
anthem was a major production, and the choir
director was quite a showman. After one long pas-
sage, he swung his long baton with a flourish, to
guide the singers onward.*

*But in sixth pew center young Bud Baines had a
different viewpoint. When the baton swung in its
big arc, he yelped, "Strike one!"*

+

Or how about this lad who seemingly had endless curiosity, but who may have just been given to
growing devilment? "How come," he asked the
preacher one day, "King Solomon couldn't afford
a bed for himself, even though he was very
wealthy?"

"Now why would you ask such a thing as that?"
the surprised minister demanded.

The boy shrugged and kept a straight face.
"Well, you just read in the Bible that 'Solomon
slept with his fathers.'"

+

At Kiwanis Club in Phoenix,
Arizona, Jack Murphy, a renowned
and reasonably honest raconteur,
reported on a boyhood friend who
is (at this writing) a fairly well
known U.S. Senator from Arizona,
the Honorable Barry Goldwater.

"When Barry was six years old," insisted Jack,
"his family was living in the Gaylord Apartments.
One day little Barry wandered off and got lost.
When police finally corralled him they asked him
where he lived.

"Young Barry looked grave, thought carefully,
and finally told the officer, 'I live in the Happy
Jesus Apartments.'"

The pastor was offering sympathy to young Barry Randall. "And were you hurt very much in the fall, my boy? The roof is quite high."

"Wasn't hurt in the fall at all. But the stop on the sidewalk broke my leg."

They were discussing the Book of Daniel. Sunday School teacher asked Johnny, "What did the magicians say?"

"They said, 'O King, live forever.'"

"All right," teacher went on, "what happened then?"

"Well, right away the king lived forever."

+

Johnny said to Bobby, "A little bird told me what kind of preacher your father is. It was a dove. It said 'Poor, poor, so-o-o-o poor.'"

Bobby considered that a moment then replied, "Well, a little duck told me what kind of doctor your father is."

+

This was back in the olden days, you've heard of them, before horseless carriages cluttered up the highways and befouled the American air. Preachers in that era got around with horse and buggy.

"Son," said this patient preacher one morning, "go fetch the old horse."

"Why the old one, Father?" Sonny countered.

Replied the good man, "My motto is, 'Wear out the old one first.'"

"Then *you* go fetch the horse, Father."

+

"If it wasn't for one of my father's important discoveries," young Harold straight-faced to his minister, "I wouldn't be here today."

Thinking to hear a heart story, the pastor asked, "What did he discover?"

He heard a heart story, sure enough. The boy said, "My mother."

The Rev. Dr. George Hunter Hall in Carmel, California, claims to have had a Chinese teakwood importer in San Francisco as one of his parishioners. His name was Chan. One night Chan heard a noise in his warehouse, so he took a flashlight and investigated. He found what appeared to be a huge bear with feet like a human boy, and the bear was carrying off a bag of teak.

Did good Presbyterian Chan then shoot? No sir, he did not. He was a kindly Chinese, he simply played that flashlight on the critter and asked, "Where are you going, boy-foot bear with teak of Chan?"

+

Finally, you take little Bartholomew Jones. Unlike all other children in North America, England and Australia, he was prone to untidiness; he scattered his clothes around his room and left them there. No other child has ever done such a thing, of course. Well anyhow, one morning his mother happened into Bart's room rather early, and she was aghast.

"Bartholomew!" she opened up on him. "Who didn't hang up his clothes before he went to bed?"

Shrewd Bart gave deep thought to that question, and came up with what has to be the perfect answer.

Said he, "Adam."

+

When little Mary Judith was aged two-and-a-half, her daddy was baptized. Next day her aunt came to visit, and the little girl said, "Oh Aunt Ola, Daddy was advertised last night!"

Chauvinism, even right-wing extremism, has been a very unfunny problem of American congregations during recent years. Perhaps it is pointed up with less severity in this story out of a Sunday School room.

Teacher asked her class of young boys, "Who was the first man?"

One boy immediately said, "George Washington."

Teacher corrected him, "No, no, Adam was the first man."

The boy shrugged. "Well okay, if you're talking about foreigners, I suppose you are right."

+

The Sunday School teacher had lectured at length on how to get to heaven, and on how to achieve status once you arrived. So now she asked, "Who will wear the biggest crown up there?"

Young Larry Detwiler had prompt and possibly accurate answer, "The one with the biggest head."

+

The somewhat peppery and opinionated maiden lady was teaching her Sunday School class of kids. "There are many men and women in heaven already," she informed them.

Little Marcia asked, "Then how come we don't see pictures of men angels with beards?"

Replied the teacher, "That is because so many men get there by such a close shave."

+

11

HOW WAS THAT AGAIN?

The preacher's gifted second-grader, Peter, left his science books one night and accosted his mother — "Didn't you tell me that the stork brought me?"

"Yes, Darling," said Mom.

"And you said I weighed nine pounds?"

"Yes."

"Well, from what I just read, a stork hasn't the wingspread necessary to carry a nine-pound load."

+

A Sunday School teacher asked her class, "Explain the meaning of this sentence — *Sufficient unto the day is the evil thereof.*"

Even the most astute adult theologians have wrestled with that one. But it was no problem for ten-year-old Barry Randall. Said he, "It simply means that the evil connected with the present time is enough without any more!"

+

The little boy and his mother were tourists in New York. They got to the Empire State Building. Up, up, up went their elevator. Stomachs and ears began to react.

At about the sixtieth floor the lad clinging to his parent asked in some desperation, "Mommy, does God know we are coming?"

One Friday the teacher at school asked her class, "What is a prime minister?"

She was startled by what had to be accepted as an accurate answer — "A prime minister is a preacher at his best."

The preacher accosted Willie Jones one Monday "William, I am told you went to the ball game instead of to church yesterday."

"That's not so!" Willie denied indignantly. "And I've got the fish to prove it!"

+

This was a youth meeting in July under the stars in the church patio, and the preacher had a nice little game going. The boys and girls would ask him a question, and he would answer it with a quotation from the Bible.

Several questions were answered with real cleverness. But in the dim light there, the class suddenly observed a night bug fly into the preacher's mouth, and inadvertently he swallowed it.

The class observed this incident, and one boy spoke right up, "How do you explain that, Parson?"

The good man was undisturbed. He smiled and answered, "He was a stranger and I took him in."

+

"What is a layman?" the minister asked his young son during a home lesson period.

Sonny had correct answer — "A layman is a pedestrian who jumped too late."

Memorable question, worth repeating, as propounded by a six-year-old American lad, "Daddy, why didn't Noah swat both flies when he had the chance?"

+

The family had returned from church service. At dinner table, they began analyzing it. Father said the sermon was poor. Mother said the choir was off key today. Uncle Henry said the organ needed tuning. Sister criticized the altar flowers.

Finally little Harold spoke in defense — "I think it was a pretty good show for only a nickel."

+

Let this be a lesson to all of you readers who tend to neglect regular church attendance. Somebody asked little Willie Jones what church he belonged to, and he replied, "I am a Seventh Day Absentist."

+

"If Paul were here today he would be regarded as a most extraordinary man," declared the parson rather pompously, lecturing the Juniors in Sunday School.

"He sure would," one too-bright lad agreed. "He'd be over nineteen hundred years old!"

+

Guests had come to little Walter's home to play many times. Finally one asked him, "Why does your grandpa just sit there reading the Bible all day?"

Replied Walter, "He's cramming for his finals."

Pastor Bill Eckel was only trying to be helpful. He asked the class of ten-year-olds if any one could repeat a commandment with only four words in it.

"I can," piped up Tommy Thompson. "Keep Off the Grass."

+

The preacher had come to dinner. But because he had a boil on the back of his neck, he was wearing his clerical collar open. He felt called upon to explain.

"We must endure such things with patience," he intoned, gently touching his neck. "We all must suffer, and we need to, as a part of our Christian discipline."

Six-year-old Buster couldn't take that. "If you think we *ought* to suffer, Dr. Hall," said the boy, "why don't you just button your collar?"

+

This preacher's son was recalcitrant, and Pop was chiding him: "Didn't you promise me to behave yourself, Son?"

"Yep. I mean, yes, Sir."

"And didn't I promise to punish you severely if you didn't?"

"Yes, Sir. But since I have broken my promise, you don't need to keep yours."

+

This was the advanced class in Sunday School, and teacher was examining the pupils. "Who can tell me where Philadelphia is?" she asked. She meant the Biblical city, of course.

But one lad replied at once, "They're playing a double-header in Chicago today."

The bus driver, himself given to strict honesty, glared at the biggish little boy. "You say you are only six? When will you be seven?" The man felt that an additional half-fare was due.

Perhaps it was, too. For the boy replied, "As soon as I get off the bus."

The preacher was giving the primary class a talk about flowers and making a moral lesson of it. Eventually he questioned them, "Now who can tell me what makes the flower grow from the seed?"

"God does it," little Roscoe dutifully answered. "But fertilizer helps."

+

A young Sunday School teacher asked one of her pupils what prejudice is.

One lad answered with singular wisdom, "It's when you decide some fellow is a stinker before you even meet him."

+

In Hazleton, Pennsylvania, Mrs. Neal Steward was telling her Sunday School pupils about Moses in the bulrushes. As a good teacher will, she probed for any loose ends.

"Come to think of it," said she, "what *are* bulrushes?"

One small boy had prompt reply, "They are papa cows in a hurry!"

+

In the minister's study one day, his small son asked, "Daddy, how did Noah spend his time when he was in the Ark?"

Pop was very busy preparing next Sunday's sermon, hence wasn't on guard as he normally knew to be. "Oh, I suppose he spent a lot of time fishing," he replied.

"What?" yelped sonny. "With only two worms?"

+

The Sunday School teacher had ranged afar. She asked her class of young folk, "Who was Atlas?"

"A giant who supported the world," replied one bright lad.

"That's right!" she was surprised. "But — who supported Atlas?"

She felt sure she had him there. But no — "He must have married a rich wife," replied Junior.

+

After a stiff lesson about sending money to missions and tithing and all that, the Sunday School teacher asked her pupils to write an essay titled "What I Would Do If I Had A Million Dollars."

All but one member began to write at once. Larry Detwiler simply locked his fingers behind his head and stared happily off into space.

Presently the teacher took up the papers, and said, "What about you, Larry? Everybody else has written an essay, but you have done nothing."

Larry grinned and replied, "Well, that's what I'd do, if I had a million dollars."

+

This teacher was being obtuse, actually giving a quiz on the lesson.

"It is wrong to work on Sunday," said a small boy in class.

"Why is it?" Teacher probed. "Policemen work on Sundays, and surely they go to Heaven, don't they?"

"No," replied the boy decisively. "They are not needed up there."

It was near Thanksgiving. Mother was showing young Junior pictures of Pilgrims going to church and telling him about the trouble with savages. "See here," she pointed. "You must be like those grand people. They went to church every Sunday."

"Well I would too," agreed Junior, "if I could carry a rifle and shoot turkeys on the way."

+

And at Clairton, Pennsylvania, reports Elder Ellis H. Shimp of the Wilson Presbyterian Church, a group of dogs remained silent on the curb in front of the sanctuary one Sunday. They just sat there listening attentively to a big hound out in the street, who was barking vociferously.

Some young folk walked by and one said, "That hound must be their preacher."

+

"No Parking Except On Sundays," read a sign on a church parking lot. A small boy added, *"Violators will be baptized."*

+

"The king was a very mean and wicked man," the little girl told her preacher father one evening.

"What king, dear?" he asked.

"The one in the Bible; the one you told about in church this morning, the one that used to run over people with his motor cars."

That stumped the preacher. "Surely I didn't say that!"

"Oh, yes, you did, Daddy. You said the king ground down the people with his taxis."

12

PASTORAL GUIDANCE

In Los Angeles sweet Miss Gloria Fancher, age five, often heard the TV announcer tell folks simply to phone for help in time of trouble. She had learned her numbers up to 10 and yearned to use them. One day poor Gloria had great trouble with her father. So she slipped into the den, alone. She dialed the first number she saw on top of the phone pad — the church!

That's the best place to go in time of stress, to be sure. The young pastor answered and listened to her somewhat incoherent account of what sounded like an emergency. In haste he back-tracked the call via another telephone, with the kind help of the telephone company's emergency service. Then off he rushed to the Fancher home.

He quickly resolved Gloria's trouble, too.

She had wanted to watch the cartoons on TV, whereas her daddy said "no". He wanted to watch the news!

+

This next pastor had taught his son well. But at school the history teacher demanded, "What did the Puritans come to America for?"

Ronnie Powers, the minister's son replied, "They came to worship in their own way, and to make everybody else do the same thing."

+

A little boy approached his pastor and solemnly spoke, "Thank you for the book of Bible stories."

The pleased minister smiled and said, "Oh that's all right, it wasn't anything much, Johnny."

Replied Johnny, "That's what I thought, too, but Mom said she'd lick me if I didn't thank you just the same."

It was a cold winter day, and a blaze crackled in the fireplace of the little one-room country church. The preacher, doubling as a Sunday School teacher, was standing before the fireplace addressing the young-sters.

"Never, never speak before thinking," he counseled, "lest you cause yourself grave trouble. That is the teaching of The Bible. It is well to count to fifty before saying anything important, and to one hundred before saying anything *very* important."

Mighty fine guidance, of course; good for all of us. Except . . .

He went on with his discourse there, but after about ten minutes the whole class suddenly began to count aloud rapidly and in unison. He paused, and finally asked what was the matter. Soon they came to the answer —

"Ninety-seven, ninety-eight, ninety-nine, one hundred your coat tail is on fire, sir!"

+

Good pastor Joseph Warner was out for a Sunday afternoon stroll through the woods, communing with nature and, no doubt, meditating on serious things. He came onto a barefoot boy with cheek of tan, and this boy was holding a pole with a line reaching into the water.

"Ah, sad, sad," the preacher scolded gently. "What would your father say if he knew you were fishing on Sunday?"

"You kin ask him," replied the boy, "He's fishin' right around the bend over there."

Now we think of George Hall, the kindly Presbyterian minister, who was also a good sportsman. One day he went up the creek to get a few fish. Near him a small boy was fishing, also. Presently, he heard the boy burst out in a blazing string of cuss words.

"Now, now, sonny," purred good Dr. Hall, "Don't you know you can never catch any fish if you swear that way?"

The scowling lad replied, "I know I ain't very good at it, mister. Here, you take my pole and use the *good* cuss words. There's some big trout in there!"

+

The preacher was giving his morning sermonette to the children down in front — you know, one of those bits that is liked by doting grandmothers. He was straining to make a point about bad habits. So presently he asked the kids, "What is it that is so easy to start and so hard to stop?"

After a short silence, one lad gave a correct answer — "Eating."

+

Young Peter Ehrhardt came home from school one day and said to his preacher-dad, "Father, one of the boys on the football team said I talk and act just like you."

"Ah," beamed the distinguished Dr. Ehrhardt happily, "and what did you reply to the lad?"

"Nothing," grinned Pete, heading quickly for the door. "He's bigger than I am."

13

PITY THE POOR PARENTS

Pastoral guidance is one thing, parental guidance is another. Time was, when parents *could* guide their offspring, and did so; those are referred to now as The Good Old Days.

+

Very often our children develop a moral point even when they are discombobulating us. This young daughter was being very boisterous, while her father was trying to read a book on world affairs. In desperation he cut a war map from a magazine, cut it into many pieces and told the girl to sit down and put this puzzle back together again. She was delighted at the prospect, and papa felt that she would be quiet for at least two hours.

In fifteen minutes she was back, with her puzzle all put together perfectly again, on top of a big board.

"How in the world could you do that so fast?" he exclaimed. "There were hundreds of little pieces."

"It was easy," said she. "You see, Daddy, on the other side is a picture of a man, so I just put *him* together properly then turned him over. And if the man is right, the world always comes out right, too. Doesn't it, Daddy?"

+

Kids can still come up with the most unbeliev-
able questions. Young Ned had been in Sunday
School long enough to know better, but one
Sunday after church he asked his Dad, "Was the
first deviled ham made when the evil spirits entered
the swine, like our lesson said today?"

+

It was soon after supper. The preacher and his
seven-year-old Charles were in the living room, reading the evening paper. Mother and sister were in
the kitchen washing dishes.

CRASH! A bunch of dishes obviously had fallen
to the floor in there. But this was followed only by
silence.

"Mother did it," said young Charles.

"How do you know?" Father asked.

"Because she isn't saying anything."

+

Harken to this enlightening conversation:

"Father?"

"What is it, Son?"

"Is there a Christian flea?"

"What in earth are you talking about?"

"The Sunday School lady read it from the Bible,
'The wicked flee when no man pursueth.' "

"Oh Son, that means that wicked *men* flee."

"I getcha. Then there is a wicked woman flea."

"No, no! It means that the wicked *flees;* run
away."

"Why do they run?"

"Who?"

"The wicked fleas."

"No, no! Don't you understand? The wicked
man runs away when no man is after him."

"Oh, is there a woman after him?"

"For heaven's sake, Son, go to bed!"

Then there was Marjorie, who had been praying for a baby sister, without results. One day her mother read aloud from the local paper, "I see here that Mrs. Watson has a baby daughter."

"In the paper?" cried Marjorie. "I'm going to stop praying and begin advertising."

Another minister, The Reverend Roy Shepler, called at a home, and five-year-old Jennifer welcomed him into the living room because Mother was on the telephone.

To open conversation as well as point up the grandeur of *mother love*, Mr. Shepler said to the child, "Now just who is it that shows you the greatest kindness, has the sweetest smile for you, gives you goodies to eat, tucks you into bed at night, hears your prayers, and"

He got no farther. Mother, overhearing the conversation as she hung up the phone, now heard her daughter's devastating answer —

"Our babysitter!"

+

Sometimes, though rarely, the parent does come out on top of a conversation with the offspring. Pretty, little Tempe Lee, aged five, daughter of minister John B. Earl, Church of the Redeemer in Philadelphia, was so dressed up for Sunday School that she queried, "Mother, what am I going to wear when I meet Jesus?"

+

"Be a good boy while I'm gone, Willie," Father commanded.
Replied Willie, "And don't what?"

+

You Moms will appreciate this. Five-year-old Junior Preston was told by his mother that God makes bad people good. Replied Junior, "Yes, I know God does it. But believe me, mothers help a lot."

Davey Detwiler, age six, came home obviously having been in a fight. His Mother jumped him. "Shame on you, Son. Don't you remember what the Bible says about turning the other cheek?"

"I c-c-couldn't," sniffled Davey. "He d-didn't hit me on a cheek, he h-hit me on the nose and I only got one!"

+

Mrs. Ellen McCoy, teaching in the Methodist Church at Shelby, North Carolina, had naturally mentioned how Jesus takes care of little folk. One day in class a little girl spoke out, "Miss Ellen, I want to learn all I can about Jesus today, tomorrow, Tuesday and Wednesday, because Thursday we go on our vacation."

+

Mother was teacher, and she asked her four-year-old Mary Ann, "Who made us?"

Mary Ann replied correctly, "God made us."

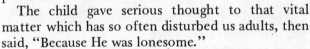

"Why did He make us?" Mother pursued.

The child gave serious thought to that vital matter which has so often disturbed us adults, then said, "Because He was lonesome."

+

Many children don't understand or don't hear too well. Up in Connecticut, little Sue was asked to give the Lord's Prayer, so she began, "Our Father who art in New Haven, how did you know my name?"

The family was touring the Rocky Mountains. Far up above Estes Park, Colorado, they had motored through the clouds, up, up, up above the timber line. Here the road got narrower and narrower and higher and higher, and there was a 4,000-foot drop-off on the right.

"Mommy," piped out little Sara Sue, "can we see God from up here?"

Before mother could answer, ten-year-old Jamie, a realist, replied correctly, "No, but if Daddy gets one inch nearer this ledge, we will!"

+

The Reverend Dr. William Boice called at a home. Mother and four-year-old Buster welcomed him into the living room; then the phone rang, and mother went to answer it. The preacher made conversation.

"My young man, do you say your prayers every night?"

"Oh, no, sir," replied Buster. "Mother says them for me."

"Ah. And what does she say?"

"She says, 'Thank heaven you are in bed.' "

+

The little girl had known poverty. Naturally; she was a preacher's daughter. So when school teacher asked every child in her sixth grade to write a short story, this child's yearnings got mixed up with her experiences. Her story began:

"Once upon a time there was a very poor preacher's family. The daddy was poor. The mother was poor. The children were poor. The chauffeur was poor. The cooks and maid were poor. The butler was poor. The gardener was poor. Everybody was poor."

Six-year-old Sharon Detwiler finally reached a breaking point. She asked, "Mother, was our baby brother sent down from heaven?"

"Of course, darling."

Sharie sighed and said, "Then I guess they must like to have everything nice and quiet up there."

+

Parents? ... They are people, said the minister, who bear infants, bore teenagers, and board newlyweds.

+

The preacher called at the Pedrick home. Thinking to stress the Christmas story, he asked the two small sons, "What is the most important thing that has happened in all of history?"

Silence, while wheels of thought turned. Suddenly little Ben Pedrick, a golfer's son, spoke out eagerly, "I know, I know! Last week my daddy made a hole in one!"

+

Father was not quite the handsomest man in town; in fact, he was somewhat the opposite. His small daughter was sitting in his lap studying his visage. Finally she spoke.

"Daddy, did God make you?"

"Of course, darling."

"Well then, did He make me, too?"

"He surely did."

"My, my, He certainly is doing better work lately, isn't he?"

It was time for Jimmy, the minister's son, to have his tonsils out. "All right, then," he agreed. "But Mommy, when I go to the hospital, I don't want them to give me no yelling baby brother like they did you. I want a puppy."

+

"Daddy, Daddy!" cried little Margie Merrick, the preacher's child, "our cat has gone to the hospital and gotten herself kittens, and I didn't even know she had been baptized, much less married!"

+

When pastor Bill Vogel came home for supper one evening, he found his seven-year-old son in tears. "What's the trouble, Jimmy boy?"

"I j-just had a ter-terible scene with your w-wife!"

+

Good Reverend Dr. Crumbworthy patted the small boy on the head and asked, "And what will you do, my lad, when you get as big as your father?"

Said the boy, "If Mother has anything to say about it, I'll diet."

+

The new baby had been squalling all week. Six-year-old Davey finally had enough of it, and spoke to his mother, "Did little brother come from heaven?"

"Yes, Dear."

Davey shrugged. "No wonder they booted him out."

14

HOW ARE THINGS UP THERE, GOD?

Of all the endless variety of activities developed by children, none opens avenues of humor more wonderful than the simple process of communicating with the Lord. "Hi up there, God, old pal," prayed little six-year-old Walter Mark Henshaw, of Dallas. "How are things with You? I'm fine, and I don't need nothin', sir. If You want anything down here, You just let me know. Yours truly, Walt." And who can say that our Lord wasn't pleased? Prayer does not require polysyllabification sonorously intonated by rabbi, pastor or priest; "Remember this," said the Master (Luke 18:17) "Whoever does not receive the kingdom of God like a little child shall in no way enter it."

+

Grandmother had bad rheumatism, which got worse whenever the weather was damp and cold. "Maybe you should ask God to send warm, dry weather for Grandmother," Daddy said to little son, Jim.

Jimmy didn't even wait for bedtime. Then and there he got down on his knees, closed his eyes, folded his hands and prayed, "Please, dear God, make it hot for Grandma."

Of course, the small fry can misunderstand us very wise adults at times. You take little Scotty Henderson who lives in the holy land (that's also down there around Dallas, ma'am). Naturally, he was being briefed on the late war between the states, and of course being given a completely unbiased version from the Southern point of view. (Don't anybody get mad here; remember, this is a fun book). Well, anyhow, Papa Henderson told him all about the great General Robert E. Lee, the great General Stonewall Jackson, all that. And, being fair minded, Papa happened also to mention the obscure general named Grant.

Right off, little Scotty piped up, "Is that the same Grant we pray to in church, Daddy?"

Now that was a stumper, and both Mr. and Mrs. Henderson looked at Scotty in surprise. "Pray to in church?" asked Mama Jean. "Surely you must be mistaken, dear."

"No I'm not, either," the bright lad insisted, "We always pray, 'Grant, we beseech thee, to hear us.'"

+

Governor Jack Williams of Arizona grew into prominence as a radio announcer. One bedtime he was with little son Rick, and overheard this surprising sign-off to prayer, "We have run out of time, dear Lord, but please tune in again tomorrow night to see what we need and hear another prayer. Thank you and good night."

+

Sweet little Lynette was concluding her nightly prayer — "Please God, take care of daddy and mother and granddaddy and grandmother and sister and brother and the baby. And be sure to take care of yourself, too, God, or else we are all sunk!"

Six-year-old super-energized Davey Detwiler of Los Angeles, son of two graduates of the University of Southern California, had been taken to see the USC Trojans play football against their arch rival, UCLA. Still excited, he nevertheless agreed to say the prayer of grace at dinner table that night; and who among us can say that the Lord didn't smile in approval? Davey bowed and spoke clearly, "Thanks for this food and bless us here at table. We hope you give us some more when you are able. Rah-rah-rah. Lord-Lord-Lord!"

+

Many millions of us males sympathize with little Rockey Rawlings, who was overheard praying just after supper, "And please, dear God, put the vitamins in pie and ice cream and cake and candy, instead of spinach and carrots and cod liver oil. Amen."

+

On December 24, little Carol Rider in Ojai, California, of course was very excited over the big day to come tomorrow. That night in her bedtime prayer her mommy heard her say, "And Merry Christmas to You, God. Amen."

+

Nanny Lee was three years old when her parents installed a new radio. She listened avidly to everything, most of that first day. That night, kneeling beside her little bed, she concluded her evening prayer thus:

"Listen in tomorrow night at this same time, God, when there will be another prayer."

Eight-year-old Lili Marie had been to adult church with her parents, and took a dim view of the preacher's long, long prayer. The preacher had come home with them for Sunday dinner, and of course he was asked to pray at the dinner table! Lili Marie felt desperate about it.

But lo, the minister this time spoke only a quick few words, then said, Amen.

Lili looked up at him and said, "It makes a difference when you are hungry, doesn't it?"

+

Shariebunny Detwiler was in bed with a sore throat. "Now darling," said Rosie her mommy, "say your prayers and ask God to make you well."

"But Mommy," countered Shariebun, reasonably enough, "isn't that what we are paying Dr. Wilson for?"

+

Apocryphal prayer by a very modern youngster: "Lead us not into temptation — we won't have any trouble finding it."

+

Louellen, aged seven, went to visit her four boy-cousins in the country; then she came home and reported, "Mother, those boys pray for God to make them good."

"How nice!" purred Mother.

"Yes," said Lou grimly, "but He hasn't done it yet."

Then there was sharp-brained little Ricardo, sitting like an angel in the pew beside his mama and daddy for twenty minutes of sermon. But his mind was exploring. When the preacher paused for a dramatic moment of silence, Rick asked loudly, "Daddy, where do the people in heaven go for a vacation?"

 Eight-year-old Wendy's grandmother was getting a bit strict. "She doesn't hang up her clothes, you do it for her," Grandmother chided the mother, in the child's hearing, "She must do things for herself."

When it came Wendy's turn to say grace at table that night, she thanked God for everything and everybody, except one. "Never mind about Grandmother, she prayed, "she can pray for herself."

+

At age four, Peter was being taught to use his own words when he prayed. Tonight he did very well, too, until he reached the end. So he peeked up and asked, "What do I say now, Mommy?"

She murmured, "Whatever you like, darling."

Pete thought a moment then closed out with, "Well good-bye, God, see you tomorrow."

+

A television star had three small girls whom she taught to pray. One night she had trouble getting them to bed, after they had listened to her program. But prayer time did come, so she listened in and heard this:

"God bless Mother and Daddy. God bless television. We are running a little late tonight, so good night, God."

+

This was Sunday dinner time, and little Harry was already at table, hungry and waiting for his dad, while also preparing himself to say the prayer of grace. Finally he called out loudly, "Daddy, for heaven's sake hurry up! I don't want to waste any more of God's time."

Then there was little Gloria. She had been doing reprehensible things, and so was sent to her room "to think it over and pray about it."

Half an hour later she came out and reported, "I thought and thought, then I prayed about the matter."

Mother's heart melted. "That's wonderful, Darling. Surely that will help you to be good."

"Oh," said Gloria, loftily, "I didn't pray for God to make me good. I just asked Him to help you put up with me."

+

Young Marcia wasn't too popular, so when her class at school planned a picnic they neglected to invite her. She said nothing. Later, the class relented and on the morning of the outing they did invite her. "It's too late," she informed them. "I have already prayed for rain."

+

Freddie's mother had taught him to remember all his kinfolk whenever he prayed. Tonight, he omitted the name of his favorite Aunt Nell, and of course Mother asked, "why?"

"Well, because," said he, impatiently, "I don't have to worry about her any more. She's engaged."

+

As the Sunday School collection envelopes were put into the basket, the pre-school class normally sang the song which included the phrase, "We will thank the Father for the gifts He sends."

Four-year-old Lawrence misunderstood a bit. Doing it solo, he sang, "We will thank the Father for the fifty cents."

Dr. Ronald Bridges, of Sanford, Maine, and Tempe, Arizona, was a distinguished Moderator of the Congregational Churches in America, and he reported on his four-year-old Danny. At Tempe, one August day, the family had gathered for dinner in 110-degree weather, and started eating without saying grace. Half way through, Danny called attention to the lack. In the oppressive heat, Dr. Bridges asked, "Well, what do you want to do, say it now?"

"Yes," replied Danny.

So everybody dropped their knives and forks, feeling a bit ashamed, of course, while Dr. Bridges led the family in a rather grim recital of their thanks.

When he had finished, Danny blithely looked up and said, "You know what that was, Dad? That was a brief pause for station identification."

+

One day Catholic churches throughout Arizona's Valley of the Sun featured a tape recording of a sermon by the bishop who lived in a distant city. When he heard the good bishop's voice seeming to come from high in the ceiling, and saw no preacher anywhere down front, one small lad in St. Theresa's Church shouted out, "Hey, is that God talking?"

15

JUNIORS ARE EAGER

Junior saints don't always understand but they are eager. This little Presbyterian girl was taken to visit an Episcopalian service for the first time. Presently she was astonished to see everybody suddenly kneel and bow their heads.

"Mommy," she piped up, loud enough to be heard all around, "what are they doing?"

"Sh-h-h-h-h-h," replied mother, "they are saying their prayers."

Daughter didn't *sh-h-h-h-h*. In even louder voice she asked, "What, in all their clothes, not in their nighties?"

+

Modern hepcat, Ricky Turek, who spent much time enjoying TV, was full of devotion or something tonight. He prayed at length. Finally he turned to his mother and said, "Mom, do you suppose it will be okay if I put in a commercial about a new two-wheeler?"

+

"Do you say your prayers every night, my little man?" asked the calling minister.

Replied the boy, "No, sir. Some nights I don't want nuthin'."

(Don't fail to grasp the moral in this for all of us, you adults!)

 Erin O'Reilly was fed up with her papa; he hadn't given her any of the three or four special pleasures she had connived for that day.

So at evening prayer time, she was overheard getting her revenge, "And please God don't give Daddy any more children. He doesn't know how to treat the ones he already has."

+

Children are not notoriously patient, and God is not notoriously as prompt as we often think He should be. Ask little Sam Goldstein. One night his mother heard him say at prayer time, "Please, dear God, make that gentile, Jimmy Jones, stop throwing rocks at me. By the way, God, I have mentioned this before!"

+

Little Oswald, saying his bedtime prayers, put in a trenchant finale: "And dear God, bless Mother and Daddy out on their party and let them have a good time. I mean, if they aren't too old for that sort of thing."

+

Here is the story of the famous little Louise, who, after living in a happy-go-lucky household, went to visit a very strict uncle and aunt. All day there, it seemed, she was getting into trouble. After one especially trying day, she knelt at bedtime and prayed, "Dear God, make all the bad people good, and all the good people easier to live with."

The Smith household was full of radios, and young Walter listened constantly. When the preacher came to dinner, Mother asked Walt to say grace. He bowed and said, "We thank thee, God, for this food and all thy blessings Amen and FM."

+

Eleven-year-old Erin was almost through with her nightly prayers, being heard tonight by her beloved daddy. She said, "And please bless Daddy and bless Mother and bless sister Robin, and please make Phoenix the capital of New Mexico. Amen."

"Why Erin!" exclaimed Daddy. "Why would you ask that?"

"Because," explained practical Erin, "I put that on my examination paper in school today."

+

Nine-year-old Mark had been having sessions with the doctor, and didn't like it. Tonight he prayed, "And God, if you are figuring to send us a baby brother, don't bother to put in any tonsils. They'd just have to be took out when he got down here."

+

Jeannine, the sweet little Baptist, was dutifully saying her bedtime prayers, "And dear God, when I am bad, please try to make me a good little girl. And if at first you don't succeed, try, try, try again."

+

Six-year-old Tommy Blevins had been out on the town; specifically, he attended a party that lasted long past his bedtime. Pooped out, sleepy, he undressed, ducked into his 'jamas and popped right into bed.

"Aren't you going to say your prayers?" Mrs. Blevins asked.

"Mom," rumbled Tom from under the covers, "I wouldn't think of waking God up at this hour."

+

The twelve-year-old rebel sullenly asked at table, "Why do we have to pray for our daily bread? Why don't we just pray for a month's supply at a time?"

His nine-year-old sister has the correct answer, "Because, silly, that's so it will be fresh!"

+

"The Sunday School teacher said something nice about me in her opening prayer before our class this morning," reported little Raymond Forcher at home.

"What, Dear?" mother asked.

"He said, 'We thank thee, O Lord, for our food and Raymond.' "

+

"Do you say your prayers before all your meals?" probed the pastor of the little boy.

"No Sir, we don't need to. My mom's a really good cook."

The small children in the Ansen household had
been praying for a baby sister or brother, and sure
enough they were soon told to expect one. But the
family went camping the next weekend. Even
there, young Travis in his tent prayed for God to
send a new baby, then ducked into his cot bed.

After a few minutes he leaped out of the covers,
knelt in the cold again, and added a postscript, "I
forgot, God. Better not send the baby to our house
tonight, Sir, because there isn't anybody there to
take care of him."

 Little Missy ran into her parents' bedroom before dawn, calling, "Mother, Daddy, what day is today?"

Daddy sleepily peeked out at her and replied, "It's Saturday, Missy."

"Oh boy," yelped Missy, "I have been praying every day for Saturday to come, and my prayers have finally been answered!"

+

Two small boys were bragging. Said one, "My pop is sure religious. Before every meal, he bows his head and says something important."

"Mine says something important, too," replied the pal. "Only he don't bow his head."

"What does he say?"

"He says, 'Go easy on that steak, boys. It's a dollar sixty a pound.'"

+

Young Robin, a sweet Presbyterian, somehow made friends with Louise, daughter of wealthy non-believers. Robin brought Lou home for dinner one night. At table, Robin's daddy bowed his head and spoke some words in low, reverent tones.
While the roast was being carved, Lou asked her friend, "What was your daddy saying there?"

"He was saying grace."

"What's grace?"

Robin looked appalled. "Why, it's the way we thank God for our food. Doesn't your daddy do that?"

"Oh no." Lou was quite lofty with it. "We pay for ours."

+

Another radio announcer had a small daughter. One night the pastor came to dinner, and doting parents thought it would be cute if little Melissa said the prayer of grace. She agreed.

With all heads bowed, she intoned a fine imitation of her father's professional voice, "This meal comes to us through the courtesy of Almighty God."

+

Six-year-old Ned Preston was becoming quite a wheeler-dealer in finance, though he did lean some toward fiscal finagling. One night his father, Bill, overheard this bedtime prayer: "And dear God, if you don't let Tuffy Hogan beat me up, and do let me knock a homerun after school tomorrow, come Sunday I will give you some money."

+

Five-year-old Earl had just had a tooth pulled, which as everybody knows is the ultimate in human torture; psychology and anesthetics to the contrary notwithstanding, even if it was wiggly loose in the first place. At bedtime the lad was overheard saying to God, "And forgive us our debts as we forgive our dentists."

+

Then here is that equally significant classic, about the father who was listening to his little daughter saying her prayers at bedside.

"I can't hear you, Mary," said he.

Mary gave firm, famous, apt reply — "Wasn't talking to you."

It was the custom in this family for everybody to kneel and close their eyes during prayers. One night, after the "Amen," mother questioned six-year-old Sonny, "How often do I have to tell you that you must keep your eyes closed when we pray?"

Sonny cooled her with his reply, "How do you know I don't?"

+

A Protestant boy came home with many bruises, including a black eye. Mom asked him whatever had happened.

"Patrick O'Reilly hit me and hit me," he admitted.

"Why did he do that?"

The boy didn't want to tell, but finally admitted that he had said to Patrick, "Down with the Pope."

"Oh dear," said the exasperated mother. Didn't you know that the O'Reillys were Catholic?"

"Yeah," admitted her son, "but I didn't know the Pope was."

+

And finally, this last story may well be the funniest prayer-related situation-episode in this or any other book.

One small boy said to his friend, "I hear that your grandfather is getting deaf."

"Getting!" exclaimed the second boy. "He has already got. Why, last night he said our family prayers while kneeling on the cat!"

END